The Image
IN THE MIRROR III

The King in Me
Transforms the Man I See

JOAN T RANDALL

Published by Victorious You Press™

Charlotte NC, USA

TITLE: THE IMAGE IN THE MIRROR III

First Printed: 2023

Cover Designer: Nadia Monsano

Editor: Lynn Braxton

ISBN: 978-1-959719-04-5

ISBN: (ebook) 978-1-959719-05-2

Library of Congress Control Number: 2023904870

Printed in the United States of America

For details email joan@victoriousyoupress.com

or visit us at www.victoriousyoupress.com

TABLE OF CONTENT

DEDICATION

To all the men who have sojourned through tragedies, hardships, pain, loss, and setbacks and chose to put the work in for their healing.

WE SEE YOU, WE ACKNOWLDGE YOU, AND WE LOVE YOU, KING!

ACKNOWLDEGEMENT

This collaboration would not have been possible without the support of my fantastic team at Victorious You Press. Thank You.

To the man who inspired this book – **Douglas Myers**. Thank you for sharing your idea with me at the Image I book signing event. I pray that you find the courage to write your story because it is needed.

To Lynn Braxton, my Editor in Chief. I praise God for your gift and your leadership. Thank you for the masterful way in which you make these stories shine.

To Angela Mitchell. Thank you for being my partner every step of the way, attending all meetings, and executing everything I have ever asked during this process.

To Nadia Monsano. You see what I see when I ask you to design a book cover. That is called complete alignment. Thank you.

And last but certainly not least, to the seven brave Kings who shared their stories. Your lived experiences are now the wisdom with which you tell your stories. Lives will be changed as a result.

INTRODUCTION

JOAN T. RANDALL

The definition of a King by natural standards and according to Webster English dictionary is a male sovereign or monarch; a man who holds by life tenure, and usually by hereditary right, the chief authority over a country or people.

The definition of a King by spiritual standards expresses Yahweh's command that man has dominion over the earth. In Genesis 1:26, we see that our Heavenly Father created humankind in His image and gave man jurisdiction over his environment. But what happens when humanity loses sight of that gift and forgets about the ultimate command? Things fall out of alignment, and man loses his ability to operate in his divine assignment.

In 2020 during the pandemic, The Image in The Mirror started as a personal book. I had a spiritual experience that sent me on a quest to see myself the way God saw me. I stood in the mirror one day, and with my eyes closed, I visualized myself as an authority created in His image. I could look beyond myself and recognize the gifts assigned to me to impact the world. I also realized that every adversity, trial, setback, and unfortunate circumstance was a part of the journey designed to perfect the purpose. I wanted to share this experience with others, so The Image in The Mirror I, an anthology with twenty women, was born. When we launched that book, I thought it was a one-and-done, but Yahweh had other plans.

The vison He gave me, birthed another book, Image in the Mirror II, which was a compilation of nonfiction stories written by fifteen women and one man. The Lord didn't stop with the book, he allowed me to work with a director to produce a phenomenal documentary where I served as the Executive Producer. The launch of this book and documentary brought people from throughout the U.S. to see it. Although this was out of my comfort zone, Yahweh had shown me that I had the authority to do everything within me, and his power enabled me to do it.

At one of our book signing events, the husband of one of the co-authors approached me asking if I worked with men to write anthologies. I told him I had never thought of doing a compilation with men only, but now that he asked, I would think about it.

He said women have a way of speaking about their trauma, pain, and hurt, which helps them heal. However, men are taught to keep everything inside and to be tough, stoic, and void of emotion. He told me he would love to share his story one day so that men can recognize that it is okay to open up. That conversation launched the idea for this book. And here we are, The Image in the Mirror III-The King in Me Transforms the Man I See.

Before this collaboration, my seven anthologies have been primarily with women. I was well versed in managing those projects, but this time it was all men, and I knew I had to use a very different approach. I had to draw on a historical biblical experience before I took on the task.

Picking up my Bible, I read the story of Deborah in the book of Judges and studied how she delivered the prophecy the Holy Spirit gave her for the deliverance of the children of Israel. As a judge, she was strategic in how she handled the law. But she was also intuitive concerning matters of the military. So to fulfill the prophecy, she recruited the Military Commander, Barak, to carry out the assignment. Her direction led to a successful deliverance. I prayed for the same discernment and wisdom to execute this assignment.

The authors featured in this book range in age from 18—60+. But each story has a message for such a time as this: seven men, seven different experiences, seven different stories, seven incredible outcomes. Through their tragedy, adversity, illness, and difficult setback, they recognized a stronger force inside than what was on the outside. That force allowed them to look internally, deep into the fabric of their soul, and found the gift of who they were to the Earth—KINGS, each created by the Creator in HIS image. It was this reality that motivated their transformation.

I am honored that I was chosen to be the vessel through which this excellent assignment was executed.

HIS LIGHT STILL SHINES: LIVING FOR DJ

DWON L. FIELDS, Sr.

The phone rang on a Friday night, and it was Kylan, my son DJ's best friend. *Why is he calling me? He has never called me before,* I thought. I picked up the phone and heard a voice speaking with urgency.

"Coach, we've been in an accident. It's bad."

I could hear a commotion in the background.

Suddenly, Kylan's mom was on the phone saying, "Coach, you need to get here!"

"I'm on my way," I said, my voice trembling uncontrollably as I sensed something was terribly wrong. I quickly called Kema, DJ's mom, to let her know that DJ had been in an accident on Bluffton Parkway. I honestly thought DJ had just been in a car accident and didn't know anything beyond that. Then, I called my parents to see if they could get to the scene of the accident since I was out of town at the time, and it would be over an hour before I could get back to Bluffton. My mind was racing as I tried to think about who else I could call to see what was going on.

My friend Brian is a firefighter, and ironically, he heard the call go out. So, he and his wife went to the scene before I had a chance to call him. When they arrived, they called me.

"Dwon, I'm at the scene of the accident, and you need to get here as soon as possible!"

"I'm driving as fast as I can, Brian. What happened?"

"I'm not sure. Just get here!" he said and hung up the phone.

I couldn't help but wonder what was going on. Everyone kept saying it was urgent, but no one was giving me details. As I made my way back to Bluffton, my phone kept blowing up. I was driving like a bat out of hell and eventually pulled up to Bluffton Parkway and SC 170, only to find the cops had the road blocked. I jumped out of the car and ran over to the police officers shouting, "My son was involved in the accident, and I need to get through the roadblock."

The police recognized me but said, "I'm sorry, Sir, but we can't let you through."

I looked at him, stunned. I knew I had to find another way to get to DJ. So, I ran back to my car and drove around until I was finally able to pull up to Bluffton Parkway from an unblocked entrance. I hopped out of the car and tried, once again, to get to the scene.

Some first responders approached me.

"My son was in the accident," I said frantically. "I need to get to him!"

"I'm sorry, Sir, your son did not make it," one of them said.

I looked at him, shocked by what he had said. I couldn't process those words, *"your son did not make it."* I just needed to find the rest of my family, especially Kema, DJ's mom, so we could get to the bottom of this. I frantically began searching for them. While I was still trying to wrap my head around what was going on, an officer approached me. He said there had been gunshots reported before the accident. I didn't know what to think or what to do. I just wandered around the scene for hours. Finally, I left and went home with family and friends.

On Saturday morning, the day after the accident, I was disoriented and in disbelief about the news I had received a few short hours earlier. I was told that a car had pulled up next to DJ's car, and someone began shooting. My son was shot, causing him to veer off the road. My son, my only son, was killed, and his friends were injured. He was only eighteen years old, a senior at Bluffton High School, and he played on the football team. He was getting ready to graduate and go to college. Why did this happen? I cried so much that I had a terrible headache.

Around 10 o'clock that morning, about twenty high school kids showed up at my door asking, "Coach, what do we need to do?" I could tell they were looking for revenge. I urged them not to do anything because retribution would not bring honor to DJ's name—it would only make things more complicated and cause me more pain, so they left.

The day got longer and longer as people kept coming by to give their condolences, check on me, and ask questions. I was exhausted and couldn't take any more, but around 7 o'clock that evening, there was a knock at my door. The Bluffton Police Department came to tell me they had two people in custody and there would be a bond hearing on Sunday morning.

Saturday night wound down, and I prepared myself for Sunday morning, not knowing what was going to happen. It was a long restless night.

On Sunday morning, as I arrived at the courthouse, I was met by family and friends waiting for court to start. It seemed like it took forever. Finally, we were allowed into the courtroom. We sat and waited for the defendants to come in.

Finally, a side door opened, and the defendants were led in, handcuffs encircling their wrists. It was then that I saw their faces for the first time. Young boys who appeared to be around my son's age. All I could do was ask myself over and over, "Why?" The charges were read, and the bond was set at one million dollars. At least I knew that the suspects weren't going anywhere for a while.

After the bond hearing, my lawyers and I spoke to detectives trying to figure out the next steps. Other names were slowly being released, and the Bluffton Police Department held a press conference. Through the tears and pain, I mustered up the strength to say, "If anyone has any information about this, please come forward. Our son was supposed to graduate June 18. He just made his college decision this Thursday. We were planning for a graduation on June 18, and now I have to bury my son." I pleaded for anybody to come forward with information.

Then, shortly after the press conference, I was notified that two people of interest were turning themselves into Beaufort County Detention Center. There was another bond hearing, and the young men's bond was denied. With the suspects now in custody, I was able to start processing what had happened.

The day came to a close, but I couldn't rest because I realized I had to plan our son's funeral. My emotions were running high; I was trying to hold it all together. Burying your own child is the worst thing a parent has to do. As I sat there, I thought *our son should be burying us; we shouldn't be planning his funeral.* That thought ran through my mind over and over again—I couldn't escape it. He had so much life to live; we never thought that we'd be saying goodbye to him at such a young age and for a reason that made no sense to us at all.

The funeral arrangements were complete; however, we were trying to figure out how we were going to keep putting one foot in front of the other. We were still in shock, and nothing seemed real.

The day of the funeral finally came with a flood of emotions. When it was all said and done, I was actually surprised that we made it through, but we had a tremendous amount of support from not just our family and friends, but also from the Bluffton community and the surrounding Lowcountry area. Saying goodbye at the funeral will go down as one of the hardest days in my life.

I knew other milestones were approaching, like prom and graduation, that would be equally difficult. It was during these events that DJ's friends really stepped up to make sure that DJ was remembered and honored. At prom, the boys made sure they had "LLDJ," which stands for Long Live DJ, sewn into their tuxedo jackets. Even though DJ didn't live long enough to go to prom, his presence was felt by his classmates and teachers.

Graduation was next, and the superintendent and principal approached us to ask if we would walk for DJ at the ceremony since he had finished his requirements for graduation earlier in the school year. We accepted and were honored to walk across that stage for our son and accept his high school diploma. The school had a special chair with a white ribbon set out just for him. When his name was called, the crowd cheered, and balloons were released; emotions flooded the entire stadium. I had such a strange feeling of joy, but it was coupled with hurt, knowing that we had accepted our son's diploma, and he wasn't able to walk across that stage himself. *He was supposed to be here at his graduation*! We had pushed him so hard to get to this day and to finish high school. As a parent, you look forward to these days of celebrating with your kids for their big accomplishments—high school graduation, college graduation, and his wedding day. Those are the days that we'll never get to celebrate.

Every day I wake up, I have so much pain, but I have to keep moving on. We know we have to put one foot forward in order to live for DJ. Everything I do and try to accomplish is for him; he's an immense part of my life and will always be with me.

Because of DJ and the way he lived his life, we have created the *Live Like DJ* scholarship fund through the Community Foundation of the Lowcountry. The scholarship was put together to help students in need of assistance with paying for college. DJ was a kid who always put others first. He was always willing to help with anything anyone asked of him. I can remember one Christmas when DJ was about ten years old. We asked him what he wanted for Christmas, and his response was he didn't want anything. He wanted to give all the toys to kids in an orphanage because he knew that they wouldn't receive anything for Christmas. So, his mother organized for him to visit a homeless shelter in Savannah, and he passed out gifts to the children who were there. Even as an elementary-aged kid, DJ had a heart for giving.

Giving and caring are the epitome of DJ. He was always looking out for others; whether it was a ride to school or a ride to games, he was always willing to lend a helping hand. This is why it hurts so much that he's gone. Losing my son, who had such a huge heart for others, is the reason that we started the *Live Like DJ* scholarships. Each year we are able to bless six young individuals with scholarships in DJ's honor. Providing scholarship opportunities is a way that we can tangibly continue to do the good work of DJ and celebrate his name.

Every day I struggle to get out of bed, but I know I have a calling to honor DJ by helping others. I try my hardest to put ten toes down, stand up, and hold my head high. It hurts like hell, but I know he would never want me to give up.

I have a mighty fight ahead of me, but I will battle every day for DJ's honor. It angers me daily to see what some young people in this country are doing—killing each other for no damn reason. It's time for us to take back our kids and teach them right from wrong. I constantly hear parents say, "I can't do anything with my child. I can't control them. They don't listen to me." My response is, "Stop making excuses! Stand up and take your kids back." They're filling up jail houses! They're filling up cemeteries! When will it stop?

The pain and anguish of seeing my son lying in a casket was the worst feeling in the world. It hurts me so much because I wasn't able to be there for him when he needed me the most. Receiving that call on March 5th started the nightmare of my life. Yet, he's the reason why I made a promise that I would never give up. I live for DJ.

Let me be the first to tell you to take every picture you can and savor every moment with your kids because you never know when it will be the last. All I have are memories of my son and the last conversation DJ and I had standing in my driveway that Friday afternoon; it was a great one. DJ has taught me so much, and I promised him that I would always have his back, so I will continue to work with our young people as my mission. I will continue to fight for DJ and any other kid that I come in contact with if they're doing the right thing. My purpose is to change our young people. I can't change them all, but I will damn sure try my hardest as I strive to keep my promise to DJ.

A MIRACLE FROM A MIRACLE

PAUL D. BUSH

When the smell of rotting flesh began to overwhelm my senses, reality began to set in. I was going to die, and I was okay with that. The first time I smelled it, I was coming out of the grocery store of the shopping center, hoping that no one else detected what was emanating from my body. The stench was staggering, so much so, that it almost brought me to my knees. I became frantic. My adrenaline started pumping. I was frustrated and didn't want to be around anyone, not even my wife at the time.

I decided to see a doctor to get tested and to receive confirmation for what I already suspected. Back then, I didn't have a cell phone, so I would have four or five voice messages waiting for me when I got home.

This went on for several consecutive weeks. But one day, I remember receiving the call I had been waiting for from a doctor to confirm my results. I heard him speaking; however, I wasn't completely listening. The doctor said they would have to do more tests and mentioned chemotherapy and other treatment options. The conversation made me angry because I refuse to die from the same chemotherapy that I knew others had died from in the past. They made chemo sound like the best thing since sliced bread. There weren't too many options back then, other than natural remedies.

I think it's important to leave this earth the way you want to, not based on someone else's ideas. At this time in my life, there wasn't really too much tying me to this world. I believed in the Holy Spirit, and because of my spiritual connection, I felt I had about an 80 percent chance of getting into heaven. However, my probability increased to 1,000 percent as the days and weeks went on. So many thoughts were running through my mind. I thought about my wife, who was unaware of what I was going through, my family, who was far away, had no clue that I was ready to die and was preparing to be with the Lord.

I became pretty good at hiding the odor. I would get home late and go straight to bed. The cover-up was definitely working. I would come in late like I had been doing, and my former wife was always fast asleep.

During the day, whether I was working or not, I spoke to God twenty-four hours per day, seven days per week. I let go of everything and everybody that could possibly keep me tied to this world. Little did I comprehend, I had just fulfilled a commandment, a New Testament scripture—one that changes the way you think and forces you to choose between the body and the spirit. I didn't even realize that I was living my life according to this scripture. But when I look back, it makes perfect sense because my priorities had changed. I focused ONLY on God, not my body or anything else. "Whosoever will come after me, let him deny himself, and take up his cross, and follow me. For whosoever will save his life shall lose it; but whosoever shall lose his life for my sake and the gospel's, the same shall save it" (Mark 8:34-35 KJV). "For what shall it profit a man, if he shall gain the whole world, and lose his own soul" (Mark 8:36)? How would I have known to do this naturally without ever reading the scripture?

Now, where was I? Oh yes, my former wife was always fast asleep, but one night in particular, as I lay on my back with my shoulders on the pillow, it felt like I was suffocating. I was in a state of shock because I was tired, and I needed to sleep. I rolled over and got out of the bed, and just stood up, thinking this was how I would die—by suffocating in my sleep. I sat on the side of the bed for about twenty minutes and prepared my mind to never wake up again. I was extremely tired, and that was the night it began. I heard the word, "sleep." As soon as my head hit the pillow, it felt like I was resting on a cloud. God put me to sleep just by speaking the word "sleep." It was a different kind of rest that I got that night.

At 4:15 in the morning, I discerned the word "AWAKE" being spoken to me. The Lord woke me up, but not only did He wake me up by simply saying, "awake," He instructed me to read specific scriptures. The Holy Spirit, thy Lord, God, Spiritual Father, whatever you choose to call a higher authority, spoke to me in a masculine voice. He spoke to me like a father teaching a son. God gave me the exact scriptures to read—the book, chapters, and verses in the Bible. This went on for over nine months straight, every single night. I will also mention the "C-word" ending with the letter "R" was not mentioned at all during this time. I was so preoccupied and focused that I wasn't thinking about my illness. I was being taught by a higher power, if you will.

The many ways I received an understanding of the scriptures I read were amazing. Sometimes it was a direct revelation. Other times, the Lord, used my bishop at a local church I had been attending back in Raleigh, North Carolina, to preach on the same scriptures that I was directed to read. Everything lined up so perfectly, causing me to begin reflecting back on my entire life.

My mother was sixteen years old when I was born. The doctor had told her that she would never have children. You see, my mother was the first true miracle. She was born with six kidneys and two bladders. To this day, I have personally never heard of anything like this. The doctors did everything possible for my mother, and because of their resolve to never give up, along with my mother's sheer determination, she overcame many obstacles. The doctors had also told my mother she would never live past the age of seven. But, of course, she lived way past that age.

My mother beat the odds in so many ways. Doctors had even told her that having children could possibly kill her, and it almost did. Not only did my mother give birth to me, she gave birth twice! She also had my younger sister who is only three years younger than me! Although they both almost died in childbirth, they are a living testimony. That was nothing but God! How else could a child born with six kidneys and two bladders go on to live a life after the doctors counted her out? To this day, my mother is still with us, AMEN.

My life, like my mother's, should be considered a miracle. You see, before I turned a year old, I picked up a bottle of my aunt's pills, Phenobarbital, and ingested them. My mother and some other family members found me on the floor, nonresponsive. They called an ambulance, and I was rushed to the hospital. I was placed into intensive care after they pumped my stomach. Later, I was told the doctors had exhausted their treatment options because the drugs were already deep in my system. So, for days on end, I lay in the hospital bed unable to move. Each day, my mother would come to the hospital after she got off work and sit by my side.

One day, while I was still unconscious, I overheard a conversation about me. There was a discussion about whether they should take me back or let me stay. You see, this was not a normal conversation; it was a spiritual one. Even though I was very young, I recall seeing two figures that were like two bright clouds above me. It still gives me chills until this day, just thinking about it. God was actually discussing my future or His plans for my life.

Later that day, my mother arrived at the hospital, as she had been doing, like clockwork, for over a week and a half. However, as she entered my hospital room, she saw that I wasn't there. She became frantic and hysterical, and then went ballistic. Just imagine your one-year-old baby who was comatose and non-responsive for almost two weeks, and now he wasn't in the room where she had visited him for almost two weeks straight. No one told her that I had awakened. So, she ran to the nurse's desk to inquire where I was. She was relieved and very thankful when she discovered that I was alive.

The doctors and nurses were also shocked that I'd actually survived. They said it was a miracle! The nurses seemed to take a liking to me because they wanted to be close to the miracle child. They kept saying that I was not supposed to be alive. Yet, here I was. They carried me around the ICU and gave me popsicles. They made me feel so special. I guess, in a way, at that moment, I was.

Even the hospital administrators agreed that it was a miracle my little body was able to survive after ingesting all of those pills. They told my mother they would not charge her for my stay in the hospital because I was a living miracle. So, my mother never had to pay a penny for the time I spent in the hospital, and that was a blessing.

Still, to this day, my mother has never forgotten this. She seems to remind me all the time. It really affected her, and I knew how she felt because

I almost didn't make it. The crazy thing is there was a second time that I swallowed some pills. Was the devil out to kill me? Both times, both bottles belonged to my mother's sister, my aunt. Why would someone leave pills lying around that a child might ingest? It seemed so irresponsible. So, due to my aunt's carelessness, they do not get along, even to this day. If it were my son, who had almost died, not once, but twice, I don't know what I would have done.

Overall, my childhood was okay, but my grandmother felt it was missing something. So, she instructed my mother to find a church for me because she said God had a plan for me. So, I went to church as a toddler by myself. I still remember my first church, the African Methodist Episcopal (A.M.E.) Church. They sent a bus regularly through our neighborhood. My mother would dress me in a custom suit and put me on the bus. When we arrived at the church, I sat on a special pew that was just for the little boys who were there to be taught one thing—discipline. Every Sunday for almost a year, I attended their service.

One day after church, when I left to go home, I jumped on the wrong bus. I was way on the other side of town, and everybody else had been dropped off except me. I still recall the grown-ups asking me for my name. After they discussed the situation, they asked me if I knew where I lived and how to get home. I told them I could show them. They were in disbelief that I was able to direct them all the way to my house, but I did. Right to my doorstep. I was only four years old, going on five, when this happened.

My grandmother always treated me differently than she did my other cousins, probably because of my near-death experiences and the fact that she believed there was something different or special about me. She also introduced me to the Holy Spirit, and my life changed. From that point on, I knew God kept his hand on me.

One day, my cousins and I were playing in another room when my grandmother called us. She gave us instructions to find a quiet place and begin to pray, just like she had taught us. I overheard my grandmother make several calls saying she was looking for my mother. She couldn't find her, and back then, there were no cell phones. I was a very intuitive child, and I sensed the stress and nervousness in her voice.

Little did I know, my mother had stopped by a friend's apartment, but no one was there. As she walked down the concrete stairs leading to the sidewalk and parking lot, a man came out of the bushes with a knife. He kidnapped my mother, took her hostage in her car, and made her drive him through the city. I think he was definitely planning to kill my mother.

It is always a blessing to have a praying grandmother, because we believe that just as my mother was driving with a knife pressed up against her side, my grandmother called us to pray. The moment we began to pray, something or someone caught this man's attention, and at a red light, my mother was able to jump out of the car and run for her life. After calling the police, she called my grandmother and told her what happened. They found my mother's car a couple of days later. The man who kidnapped my mother had set the car on fire. I'm convinced our prayers saved her life. Through that experience, I learned a lot about my grandmother and God. She taught us to always have faith in knowing God answers prayers. My biological father was never around, so if I had lost my mother, it would have been devastating for my younger sister and me.

There was never really a man around the house, so as a teenager, I was tasked with responsibilities that a father would typically have done. It was frustrating at times, but there was no one else to go grocery shopping when my mother was preoccupied with other things. I walked 20–30 minutes to the store, then walked back home with the groceries.

One day, I was so upset I began to cry. That was the moment the Lord heard my cry. I was upset about not having a father during a time when a boy needed one. I came to realize how important it would be for my son to have a father in the home. I recall telling God that he was going to be my father because I didn't have one, and I asked God to one day give me a son so that I could be the father to him that I never had. I have come to realize that we all do the best we can for those we love and care about and that we can't expect more than what we can give to those we love. You'll understand the importance of this later because God surely said yes.

As I got older, I came to realize that one day, I would leave the city I had spent my entire life in to get away from a traumatic experience that left me full of anger and rage. This anger and rage led to a hatred that affected my whole existence. Like most young adult males, I tried things that I should not have, like smoking and drinking. God had plans for me, and that was definitely not part of it. The Spirit, sometimes you call it your conscience, told me to leave those cigarettes alone. But after a while, I wasn't listening, even after I moved away from home to North Carolina, and was preparing to get married.

Living in a new city and state, away from everyone I've ever known my entire life was kind of scary. Had it not been for the Lord, I don't know how I would have dealt with the rage and anger I carried with me from home. After a number of years of being married, I became a little reckless, and I began drinking, smoking, and hanging out with the wrong crowd. I also stopped attending church.

One night, I was with my in-laws drinking and smoking. It had gotten late, and I couldn't drive home, so I remained planted on the couch at my cousin-in-law's apartment while he and some other guys left to get more to drink and smoke. It was then that I received the shock of my life. The music videos were playing on the TV, and the volume was extremely high. We were watching a continuous list of rap or hip-hop music videos. There were two other fellas who remained at the apartment with me. They were both in their own world, like me, kind of zoned out after all the drinking and smoking.

While the videos continued to play, I could clearly make out the music, but the rapping of the lyrics began to die out as if I was only listening to an instrumental. I wondered if the other two fellas were experiencing the same thing that I was, but I didn't want to ask them, as they both looked as if they were in a comatose state, not moving, just staring straight ahead. I could not hear the rappers on the video anymore, even though their mouths were moving! Suddenly, God began to speak directly to me as if I was being chastised or reprimanded. He was speaking to me at the same tempo as the music. I was amazed yet scared at the same time, if you can imagine that. I just knew I was going crazy because I don't think anyone else could hear what was audible to me. I was freaked out, so I quickly got up and left.

I thought that would solve the issue, and I would come out of this twilight zone I was experiencing. Who was I that God cared enough about me to speak directly to me like a father to a son who has lost his way? I jumped in the car, more like I stumbled into my seat with my adrenaline pumping. I was headed home. I was only three exits away. But before I could reach the first exit, I pulled over onto the median. Something sobered me up quickly, as if I had never been drinking or smoking that night. It shocked me because, just five minutes ago, I was too drunk and high to drive.

I found myself sober on the side of the road crying like a baby, asking the Lord to forgive me. It was too late because He had warned me several times. Many of us receive several warnings, but we ignore them; then, when it's time to receive what we deserve, we begin asking for forgiveness. I had some suffering to go through; I could just sense it. My punishment was coming. I just didn't know exactly what it would be. I immediately stopped smoking and drinking after that. Wouldn't most people stop after an out-of-body experience like that?

I got back into church and got my life together because I knew God was really trying to get my attention because he had something for me to do in life. I saw a glimpse of my potential through my recent interaction with God. It changed me, and my relationship with God grew even closer than ever before. My priorities changed. God was my only focus. Nothing in life even mattered to me at this point because I knew no one could help me but God.

It didn't take long after that for me to begin to exhibit symptoms that would later lead to lung cancer from the smoking damage I had caused to my own body. By this time, I was married, but we didn't have any children yet.

Several years ago, my mother approached me, intent on explaining what happens to people who smoke cigarettes.

"You know, the symptoms of smoking kind of feel like indigestion," she said. "Smoking creates air pockets in your lungs that pop and have you thinking it's indigestion, but it's not."

I clearly heard her that day, but I wasn't listening until I realized I was having the same exact symptoms that she had mentioned. I was horrified and upset with myself that I had not listened to her years before.

The conversation with my mother was all about avoiding reckless decisions because my grandmother, who had raised me, died early in life from smoking cigarettes. For most of my younger days, my grandmother was there to raise me since my mother was so young when I was born. I was very attached to my grandmother; mom is what I called her. I wish she was still here to witness the change in my life.

I began to grow closer to the Lord all over again, as I did as a child. I spent most of my days with the Lord. Everything my mother said to me several years ago about smoking and the health risks involved came rushing back to me when I began to experience intermittent pain. During this tumultuous time, the Lord occupied my mind and my heart. He used me to minister to others. Lives were changed in miraculous ways, even as my health and life continued to deteriorate.

For nine months, I endured the pain and prepared to leave this world. Until one Sunday, my life changed once again. It was a nice sunny day. I was in church enjoying the service when a voice said, "I am coming in." You see, I could hear the Lord and feel His presence; I just couldn't see Him. He told me to start praising Him. I agreed, even though I didn't quite understand. As I stood up, He brought back to my attention all the scriptures He had me read and study during the last nine months. I began to revisit scriptures that referenced the process of war in the Old Testament. There were always three trumpets to blow that had their own significance. I was one of the trumpets making noise, sounding off.

As the middle doors of the church opened, I sensed the Lord's presence as He came through the doors and down the aisle toward the altar. People were shouting as the other two trumpets were being blown to also praise His holy name. The choir members in the stands were shouting. We were all caught up in praising and worshipping the Lord.

After service, we were told that some members of the choir mentioned seeing an angel coming up the aisle toward the altar. As this angel moved through the congregation, I noticed his presence move through me as if a mighty wind had surged through my body. It was at this moment that I realized the pain had left my body. He had carried all the pain away.

I never returned to the doctor who had diagnosed me because he was not a believer, and he wanted to treat me with chemotherapy, which I didn't believe in. I saw him as an evil person. However, I did begin receiving regular checkups and bloodwork. I anxiously waited to see if anything abnormal would ever come up in my lab tests. But it didn't! Nothing. This confirmed that the Lord had miraculously healed me during the church service on that memorable Sunday morning which I will never forget.

It took a few weeks for me to get over the fact that I wasn't going to die. I was on an emotional roller coaster, full of so many different feelings. I was happy, yet I was sad. Why? Because I was really looking forward to being in heaven. I had prepared my mindset for death, not life. I learned so much from this whole ordeal—it has been absolutely amazing. My life will never be the same. I know those reading this may not quite believe every part of my story, but it's God's honest truth.

Do you want to be in God's plan? If so, then you have to invest your time and energy in connecting with Him. You must also begin to fast on a regular basis. Learn to protect your heart, meaning fill your heart with love, no matter what. This opens up the opportunity for God to interact with you on a spiritual level. Let go of anything that could interfere with an opportunity for you to communicate with God. Read His word, even if you don't initially comprehend it. He will help you to know and overstand His word. Recognize that you do have a purpose, and that purpose will connect you to God.

I began to read and study Psalms 37 and 40. It was a great place to start. Then, I moved to the New Testament and read the book of Matthew. It gave me a foundation to build upon. Over the years, God has continued to use me and teach me as well. My experiences with God have saved me many times. It was a boldness in the face of death that protected me and sustained me against the enemy.

I have to believe that if you are determined to reach God on this kind of level, it will happen. Continue to seek Him daily. He is waiting for you to come to Him. In Jeremiah 29:13 (NKJV), the Bible says, "You will seek Me and find Me when you search for Me with all your heart." Remember, He has always been near you and is trying to reach you. Psalm 145:18–20 (NIV) states, "The Lord is near to all who call on him, to all who call on him in truth. He fulfills the desires of those who fear him; he hears their cry and saves them."

Are you ready for a closer connection to God? Remember, you can only communicate with Him spiritually, but be prepared to grow and strengthen your prayer life by studying the Word.

When I was on the verge of dying, I chose God as my doctor. I was prepared to live or die with my decision. Most importantly, I never wavered in my faith. I trusted Him to handle the situation His way. And I will be forever thankful and grateful for what He has done for me. I pray that my story will inspire you to lean on Him, too, for whatever need. Seek HIM with all your heart.

CROWNED BY GRACE

JARVIS SWANSON

As I walked out of the Showcase Cinema Movie Theater, I found myself in a daze. It felt like being in a dream state, disconnected from the moment but not fully drifting away. My wife and I had just spent two hours watching Denzel Washington's directorial debut in the film, *Antwone Fisher*. During the movie, the story felt familiar and inspiring in a way I couldn't quite grasp, but the grip it seemed to have on me wouldn't let my mind rest.

For the entire twenty-minute drive, my mind retraced moments in the movie like words to a song I couldn't get out of my head. Just as I turned onto my mother-in-law's street to drop my wife off for a visit, one particular part from the movie replayed slowly in my mind. In the scene, Antwone recalls the abuse he endured at the hand of an older foster sibling in the basement of his foster mother's home. As it played in my mind, the words she spoke to him revealed a door. I questioned why the door was there since it wasn't in the movie scene. Before I could fully conceive the thought, the door opened, and suddenly these images, sounds, tastes, and memories flooded my mind with ruthless fury as if a tsunami had unleashed them.

As we pulled up to my in-law's house, I broke the unusually long silence of the car ride with an uncontrollable release of emotion. I cried so hard the tears burst from my eyes, and I could barely breathe as I recalled in vivid detail my own sexual abuse at the hands of a teenage babysitter. I was wrecked and my young bride was confused, terrified, concerned, and swimming in the deepest emotional waters she or I had ever known. We were ill-equipped for the situation we found ourselves in that night. It would take me many years to realize how that moment revealed my greatest fears and had a significant impact on our marriage.

We had only been married a couple of years before this occurred. I was two years older than her and had seen her a few times in the neighborhood. I thought she was gorgeous, light-skinned with greenish-hazel eyes and hips for days! I must admit my initial attraction was mostly physical, but as I got to know her, I learned to love how resourceful and passionate she was. I thought she was the type of person that could see problems and be willing to do something about them.

After we'd been dating for only about six to eight months, we found out she was pregnant. This would be my third child with as many women. But I wanted this to work and be different from my past relationships. I prayed for the baby every night and desired to be a better version of myself for her and the baby. I got custody of my five-year-old daughter, Jalisa, and I became more intentional about seeing my son, Jalen, who was three years old. I was making an earnest effort to be the type of man Heathcliff Huxtable, the TV father on The Cosby Show, could be proud of. It seemed like God was honoring my new devotion to my family.

On January 19, 1999, our daughter, Jhanae Tatiana, was born into the world two months premature! Due to medical complications, she had not been getting proper oxygen to her brain and developed a gene-linked malformation known as Lissencephaly, which literally means "smooth brain." The smooth surface of her brain made it almost impossible for her to store enough energy in the muscle. She could sleep for twenty hours and, after minimal activity, would be so drained that she would go right back to sleep. Here was this beautiful little bean-sized human life that could fit easily in the palm of one hand. I felt helpless and outmatched by the situation.

Three days into Jhanae's life, the lead neonatologist called us into a cold, beige, lifeless meeting room and asked a twenty-one-year-old mother and twenty-three-year-old father to make the most difficult decision imaginable about their newborn baby's life.

"Right now, your daughter's breathing is only being supported by a machine, and without that machine, she cannot sustain life. If I were you, I would take her off the machine, take her in your arms, and let her pass on," he said with clinical-like compassion, fitting for the room we were in.

I was devastated and confused, but almost like a reflex, I retorted, "My God can do anything! We will not make that decision for Him, and if He wants her, He will take her despite using the machine."

Jhanae would go on to live for five years, and while she never spoke a word beyond a deep sigh or moved her limbs beyond an intense stretch, she taught me the most important lesson of my life. Jhanae required unconditional love. She never said, "Thank you, daddy," and she never expressed to me how much she appreciated my effort to provide for her. She didn't reward my guidance and watchful eye with newly gained skills and abilities. I had to choose to love her because I knew she deserved love.

Amazingly enough, everyone around her loved her. My Aunt Mitzi dedicated her life to my daughter! She opened her home to my family and spent many mornings and evenings at Jhanae's bedside, singing, reading, and praying over her. Her nurses did her hair and nails, gave her spa days, dolled her up, and told elaborate stories on her behalf as if she had whispered them in their ears! She taught me that the power of presence is not in your words but in your ability to give and receive love, and love is a choice exemplified by actions.

Jhanae's condition and need for around-the-clock care weighed heavily on our hearts and young marriage; however, it was not what ultimately doomed it. The parasite that drained the life from our relationship hatched that night after the movie. As I was coming to terms with a horrific childhood experience, my wife was also wrestling with how to deal with my trauma. When I dropped her off at her mom's, she was attempting to get her footing after blindly stepping into emotional quicksand with me. So, she told her mother I had been sexually abused. Looking back as an older man, I completely understand why she told her mother, as I'm sure she was visibly shaken coming into the house after dealing with that experience. However, at the time, I didn't see it that way.

Just a few days later, I saw her mother, and she looked at me with every bit of sympathy she could muster.

"Oh, Jarvis, I am so sorry for what happened to you," she said softly.

I was shocked and embarrassed. I quickly looked over at her, and the level of betrayal I felt in the moment struck me to my very core. I couldn't understand how she could share something so deep. In fact, that incident was so shameful and traumatic, I buried it deep inside me for sixteen years, somehow, hiding it from myself. To that point, I had never verbalized it to anyone. As a result, I made a decision that would ultimately crush our marriage. I told myself I could not trust her. I no longer felt safe sharing the things that made me tick. This would prove to be devastating to our relationship, because what is a man but his thoughts, hopes, dreams, fears, and vision for the future? I no longer gave her this part of me.

When I needed to express frustration with life or contemplate my future, I went to my mother. I had created a relationship in which I was physically married to my wife, but I was emotionally attached to my mother. My mother became the place where I laid the treasures of my mind. Slowly over time, this was the undoing of our marriage. Many things happened before the house of cards fell, but that one decision ground the foundation of our marriage to sand.

While the air slowly escaped from the marriage, I struggled to keep up my facade of faith in God for three reasons: 1) I still had not dealt with my childhood traumas. 2) I wanted God to heal me the way I thought He should, and when and how I thought He should. 3) I was mad at God because he gave us this special-needs child, even though I loved her and prayed for her every night before she was born. I had not done that for my previous two children, so in my mind, He did this to me. The mask of a faithful Christian didn't come off all at once, as it never does. We generally don't quit and walk away all at once; it happens slowly over time. A man can spiritually and emotionally leave his family years before he physically walks out the door for the last time.

Subconsciously, I was searching for a replacement wife without telling myself that's what I was doing. It was subtle, like ivy growing up the side of a building; one day, you forget to trim it back, and a year later, you can barely see the windows and brick siding on the house. It started by comparing her attributes to other women's and how well I related to them versus her, because, at this point, "I am older and better understand what I needed." Comparison is a game with no winner. If we lust after something long enough, the person or thing appears to be better than what we currently have, but this is because we tend to only look at the evidence that confirms the decision we've already made up in our minds that we want. So, after four years of a turbulent marriage that produced two children, we separated.

At this point, I was doing things daily that I swore I'd never do. My life felt like I could be a guest on an episode of the Jerry Springer Show. I was living with the woman who would become my second wife, who had just had my fifth child, Jonathon. So, if you're counting, that's four women and five children, although, by this time, Jhanae had passed on.

In addition to the woman I was living with, there was a young lady I was entertaining on the side. In my mind, the side chick was the perfect situation. I know, bad logic, but let me explain. She was in town visiting family and scheduled to be around for about a month or so. We could hang out, smoke, and have sex without getting caught up in any emotional drama! Or, so I thought. Remember, I said I only looked at evidence that supported the decision I wanted to make. So, we finally hooked up.

About a week before she was to leave town, she called me at 3:00 am! She was hysterical and barely making any sense. I finally got her to calm down enough to tell me what was going on.

"My life is worthless," she wailed. "I can't do this. I just want to end it, right now. I can just go to sleep forever and not have to deal with anything anymore."

Hearing this, I sat straight up, I was fully awake now. But before I could ease out of the bedroom, Demetra began to stir.

"Hey, what's going on?" she asked.

I quickly made up a lie, "Sorry, it's a girl from the neighborhood. She's having a breakdown. She thinks I'm a good guy who can help her."

"Whatever," she said as she laid her head down.

I turned my attention back to the phone and quickly exited the room. This lady was crying her heart out to me. I felt ill-equipped, but that old reflex kicked in, and for the next few hours, I told her everything I could recall about the love of Christ Jesus and His desire to give her the most out of her life. By the time we got off the phone at 6:00 am, I was left asking myself a simple question, "If He is so good, why are you not with Him?"

About a month later, I was in a sunken place but didn't quite know how or why. One day, I was home alone, doing some renovations to the house my now estranged wife and I shared during our marriage. She had abandoned our home a couple of months prior. Demetra called and hit me with a series of questions for which I didn't have any good answers, and then she made a statement that shook me as if she was trying to wake me from a deep sleep.

"Jarvis, you were so much more mature when I met you. It seems like back in February you just started going down."

Now at that moment, I was not quite sure what had happened back then, but the fact that she was able to pinpoint a period of time for me to work from was like she breathed life into the lungs of a drowning man. I knew something had been off with me, but I couldn't understand why. It was like every decision I made took me deeper into the depths of my despair.

When we hung up, I was confronted with a choice that set my life's course from that day forward. Two things were clear in my mind. One, I knew I would marry this woman because, until that moment, I had never had a woman observe me to the degree that she could see the change in my mindset down to a specific time period. I felt truly seen for the first time in my life. Secondly, I knew I could not do life without God's guidance. I kept getting myself caught in these traps of my own clever decision-making.

So, I got on my knees and prayed, "Lord, I now intimately know what I am good at! I have perfected making bad choices. If You are real, show me that You can do something better with my life than I have done. I will make this commitment to You so that You can prove Yourself. If you show me what to do, I will do it. If you teach me, I will teach others." I got off my knees and knew instantly that my life was different. What I didn't realize is that while the course of my life had changed, I would have to allow God to show me how to untangle the knots and kinks I had created in the life I had created for myself.

This time in Christ would be different. The first time I tried walking with God, I wanted to lead Him, not be led by Him. This time I followed the Good Shepherd, and most importantly, I understood that I was a hardheaded, too easily lost, scared, and damaged ram. The Lord gently began to reveal how I needed to give all things to Him, including my relationship with Demetra.

One month after Demetra and I moved into the house I was renovating, the Lord spoke softly to me that we needed to stop being intimate. The problem was that we were both broken people and needed this connection to feel loved, so to stop what had sustained us for the past two years was a huge ask! However, I had committed to God that I would do whatever I felt He was leading me to do. At first, we were committed and diligent. Then, after a few weeks, we felt lonely and isolated and ran to each other for comfort. Afterwards, I felt like I betrayed the trust of a friend, my God.

The next day, I was driving along when I felt like the Lord's intimate presence lifted from me. The warm, cozy, and secure environment I had known for the past few months was gone. It was like I was completely uncovered, like an exposed nerve; I felt truly naked for the first time in my life. I started to panic and cried out in repentance to the Lord, and immediately I heard Him say, "My grace is sufficient for you!"

I cried all that day, just reflecting on that exposed feeling and never wanting to be without His presence again. Dee and I remained celibate until we were married nearly two years later. Unfortunately, Dee was not the only object of my affection. At this point, I had had a fifteen-year relationship with pornography and masturbation, and this woman-of-many-faces and silhouettes would prove to be much harder to break up with.

My first experience with pornography was when I was about seven or eight years old, looking at my uncle's Playboy magazines in the woods with my cousins. Then, at around ten years old, a few kids in the neighborhood would meet up with a friend who had an "uncle" that lived around the corner from her. When he was gone, she brought the group over to watch a triple X-rated video. This was very different from the Playboy magazines I had seen a few years prior. While I could barely stomach what I was seeing, I couldn't turn away either, partly because of the pressure of not wanting to be the only one in the group who couldn't watch and partly out of fascination. While I only half watched, the seed of sexual perversion that had been planted years prior by the hands of someone older, was poised to fully mature.

I am conflicted about whether to call the teen who sexually offended me an abuser. I wonder if he was exploring as someone had explored with him, and while I know it was violating and damaging, I also know that sexual perversion can take a young victim today and make them a victimizer tomorrow. In fact, this was my experience. Inappropriate sexual exploration was an issue in my family for at least three generations. I now know of several cousins, aunts, uncles, and grandparents who experienced sexual trauma at the hand of a relative. I did not understand that what we were doing to each other was wrong until I was thirteen.

One night, a close relative and I were up late talking, and when I began to fondle her newly developing breast under the comforter we were sharing. After a couple of minutes, I leaned over to put my mouth on them.

"Jarvis! This is wrong!" she said intensely.

As soon as she said those words, it was like a bright light illuminated the darkness of my mind, and I understood that she was right, and it could no longer be treated as normal because it was wrong. This was the last time I was ever involved in any sexual contact with anyone in my family.

However, with all the sexual trauma in my young history, it would be no surprise to become addicted to self-gratification once my first real girlfriend, at age fifteen, introduced me to masturbation during our nightly phone conversations. The combination of sexual trauma and inappropriate exposure would make pornography and masturbation my only consistent relations for the next fifteen years.

Now, I find myself in a relationship with this God who says if I look at a woman with lust in my heart, I have already moved my feet from His righteous path. I believed this in my head, but by this time, my mind was riddled with sexual imagery, and my imagination was even worse. I only saw most women as objects to be consumed and enjoyed, whether physically or in my mind's-eye. Healing in this area could only come from God. It would take some time and meticulous restoration of my heart and soul because I had to be renewed in the way I viewed women as a whole.

God started the process with repentance. This was important because the decisions I had made to engage in these sinful acts gave the enemy access to my mind. There were times I would close my eyes at night to sleep, and I could not rest because I would be bombarded with non-stop thoughts and sexual images. It was like having a television in my head showing programs I no longer wanted to watch but couldn't shut off. This meant that without my permission, the enemy would suggest things based on the choices I had made in the past. However, at the moment of repentance, my past was no longer charged to me, and the enemy would need a new agreement to have his former level of access to my mind. This did not and does not prevent him from trying to regain entry to old doors. Therefore, I am thankful the healing process has started and is maintained through my continual repentance.

The next thing the Holy Spirit had to heal was how I viewed women. I had to learn to see them as whole beings, not just objects of adoration. Understanding that I'm analytical, God gave me a logical view of His spiritual truth. He helped me to understand the spiritual implications of Matthew 5:28. To look at a woman in a desirous way without her consent or knowledge deprives her of her right to free will, a God-given gift to all humans. This is adulterous, and adultery without permission is considered rape. In other words, it is my belief that to look at and consume a woman in a nonconsensual manner and with forbidden desire constitutes spiritual rape. When the Holy Spirit showed me this picture of His truth, it was just like my relative all those years ago saying, "Jarvis, this is wrong!" Now armed with this perspective and determination not to violate women in this way ever again, I repented and asked the Lord to give me the right way to see women, because they aren't going anywhere, and they are still attractive.

The Holy Spirit honored my petition and gave me this revelation. I was not looking at my mother, sisters, aunts, daughter, or certain close friends in a sexual way, because once they were placed in that category, in my mind, it was wrong to see them in any way that was inappropriate to their position in my life. I sought to know them and understand them at a depth that was more intimate than their sexuality. I know them at the level of their humanity. He told me this is how I should look at all women, and to understand that I get one wife, and she is to be my only covenant desire. However, I could have many fulfilling and loving relationships with the women in my life, and because I now viewed them in the proper context, I could love them deeply and without shame as humans.

Since learning and living this truth, I have not looked at pornography in over fifteen years, and with clarity and purpose, I still guard my heart and mind to prevent the enemy from gaining any foothold. I also have rich, loving relationships with many women, and I set boundaries to keep them in their appropriate context to promote proper growth.

In the spring of 2007, eight members of my family representing multiple generations gathered in a room. We openly discussed the sexual traumas we each experienced and how they affected us as children and still as adults. We all made a commitment to not allow these egregious incidents to impact the future generations of our family by allowing inappropriate sexual behavior to hide and create secret places of shame and darkness from which the enemy could operate. The enemy has trouble hiding in a place where there is open and honest communication. That's why the phrase, "See something, say something," is so vital.

In my immediate family, we had two generations of teen parents. My father, mother, three older brothers, my sister, and I all had our first child at age sixteen. God will break the generational curses of His children if we obey. My first grandchild, Jace Isaiah, was born to my twenty-seven-year-old son, Jalen. Also, none of my nieces or nephews have had children before the age of twenty-one.

God continued to untangle my life. As I prayed one day, God impressed upon me that I needed to tell Demetra about the girl that called me at 3:00 am a few months back. I was very hesitant and couldn't reason why it was necessary to do that since she had gone back to her city, and I didn't see or hear from her again. Then, He lovingly breathed this thought into my spirit. He wanted glory from every part of my story! If Dee remained in the dark about it, then I could not ever share it, and if I can't share it, He can't redeem it, and if it's not redeemed, He can't be glorified through it.

After crying and bargaining, I finally worked up the courage to tell her. I was sure she would leave me because I had lied about this when she first asked me about the girl who called that night. What happened surprised me and endeared me to Dee and made me trust God on a deeper level. I told her everything, the whole truth, as the Lord directed me to. I waited for her response with bated breath.

Dee looked at me and said, "I knew you were lying about her. I'm hurt, but I forgive you, only because I am watching you change as a man right before my eyes. Back then, if you were then, the man you are now, I don't think you would have done that."

I was floored! I couldn't believe what I heard and, more importantly, what I was feeling. I felt more connected and loved by her than in any moment of intimacy we had shared prior. At that very moment, I was aware that I had experienced grace for the first time in my life. I'm convinced that God knew how she would respond, and He wanted her to give me a microcosm of His nature. Also, I believe that God has us do things out of obedience on one level, so that we have the faith and confidence to be obedient and honor His nudges and commands on the next level. I would need this confidence for the next directive!

While in prayer one day, the Holy Spirit spoke these words to my heart, "Son, you have to go back to your wife and reconcile the marriage."

At this time, I was more in love with Demetra than I had ever been with anyone. Plus, my wife and I couldn't have a conversation for more than twenty minutes without fighting about something, and both she and I have had a child with our current partners since we separated three years prior. I was confused and deeply devastated by His instruction.

After offering God all the tears I had, I finally gathered my composure enough to ask, "What about Demetra? What do I tell her?"

"You don't tell her anything." He replied. "This has nothing to do with her."

I responded with an additional offering of tears. Remembering my commitment to do whatever I felt He asked of me, I asked, "How would this even work?" I listened carefully as the Holy Spirit laid out a plan.

Later that day, I called my wife and said, "Do you want to try to make our marriage work?"

"What are you talking about?" she sounded confused.

I repeated my initial question and added, "I was praying, and the Lord told me I needed to ask if you want to try again."

This time, she raised a familiar question. "How would that even work?"

So, I told her the plan God had told me. We would both separate from our current partners, date each other for six months to rebuild the friendship, then renew our vows one year from now.

After breaking down the plan, there was a long silence on the phone. Then, in a lighthearted, almost nonchalant tone, she finally replied, "Nah, I'm good!"

When I hung up the phone, I felt better and cried tears of joy and gratitude. Through the sobbing, I heard the Lord say, "Where I am taking you, you could not give her the opportunity to accuse you of abandoning her without trying to make it work."

There have been and continue to be many other cracks, tears, and wounds the Lord is healing in me, but this was the last huge entanglement I had created that God dealt with in this new season of walking after Him.

I have now been a committed follower of Christ for sixteen years at the penning of this chapter, and I can say without a doubt that the life He has built is nothing short of a miracle. I grew up lacking in resources and hopelessly lost, but He found me and gave me direction and purpose.

Demetra and I have now been happily married for fourteen years and have partnered on some monumental achievements as a couple. The Lord has taught me how to love her and how to be loved by her. We've raised four beautiful and loving humans and have had the honor of impacting the lives of many young men and women with our story and transparency, the half of which I couldn't tell in this writing.

Over the years, I have witnessed the Lord honor my request of Him all those years ago, and He has proven Himself again and again. Therefore, I continue to trust Him for revelation and outcomes, and I have learned to trust myself with implementation. The King in me has truly created the man I see. He has given me grace and filled my life with meaning. I am a KING crowned by HIS glorious grace.

MERCIFUL HEALING

ABRAHAM ANDERSON

I thought I was invincible until one day it all came to a screeching halt when suddenly my life was turned completely upside down. I was a physically strong man, athletically inclined, and I loved to work out on a daily basis. I had even earned the Expert Field Medical and Air Assault Badge that required extensive training that is only obtained through perseverance and hard work. I, also, served as a senior non-commissioned officer in the United States Army in a leadership position, and studied graduate level classes while maintaining my responsibilities as a husband and father.

Yes, my life was very busy, but despite my achievements and status in life, most importantly, I am a disciple of Jesus Christ, who is my Lord and Savior. I serve as an usher in the church, pay my tithes and offering, and enjoy having time to fellowship with other Christians. Faith is a very important part of my life. Little did I know that soon it would be tested beyond anything I could ever imagine.

The most difficult journey of my life began when I started to experience severe and sometimes uncontrollable hiccups that affected my concentration to think or reason, and it caused confusion to where I lacked the desire to even work out. Each time they would flare up, I would go to the doctor. I couldn't understand what was happening to my body. After having these symptoms for six months to a year, they finally diagnosed me with gastroesophageal reflux disease (GERD). They explained this occurs when stomach acid flows into the tube that connects my mouth and stomach. I was given antacids to control the symptoms.

When I told my wife, Annette, what the doctor said, she commented she wasn't sure if this was an accurate diagnosis.

The Back Story

During my senior year in high school, my mother kicked me out of our home that I had lived in all my life. She was a God-fearing Christian that believed in not sparing the rod, which was often used to control nine kids. At times, I felt abused. There were many nights I slept on the front porch in freezing rain and snow. I tried to unlock the front door; however, it was bolted, I was locked out with nowhere to go. I felt unwanted, rejected, and unloved. Many years later, I can now acknowledge that my behavior and lifestyle was not pleasing to my mother's standards. I was not a bad kid, I just needed guidance and direction, which I did not get from my parents.

So, after I was evicted from my home, my oldest sister, Patricia, and her former husband, David, allowed me to move in with them until I got my act together. After I graduated from high school, my brother-in-law persuaded me to join the United States Army. That was the best decision I have ever made.

Soon after I enlisted, and had to leave for basic training. My mother met me at the train station to say goodbye. I never had a close relationship with her because of her stringent, hard love, and mentality. However, I still loved my mother, despite our differences. After a brief hug, I said goodbye, and stepped onto the train.

I headed to bootcamp at Fort Dix, New Jersey, and spent eight grueling weeks, followed by three months of Advance Individual Training (AIT) in Fort Polk, Louisiana where I learned my trade as a Physical Activities Specialist. Then, I was transferred to my first duty station overseas in the United Kingdom.

During my assignment in England, I became a borderline alcoholic. I'm not sure if it was the stress of the job or other factors, but it altered my ability to function effectively as a responsible husband and father. I knew this was not who I wanted to be, so I had to make some serious changes in order to save my marriage.

After my wife and I discussed my situation, she lovingly placed anointing oil on my forehead and prayed to God to deliver me from the bondage of alcohol. She declared that I would be saved before leaving England. Her prayers came to pass, and I gave my life to Christ. I'm so grateful I did.

Bound for Paradise

I was ecstatic when I initially found out I would be stationed in beautiful Honolulu, Hawaii. It was the duty station that everyone wanted—warm weather, blue skies, palm trees, beautiful beaches, clear blue ocean water, great food, and friendly people. Some called it "Paradise." It was going to be a nice change after dealing with the cold winters in England.

Once we arrived in Hawaii, it was easy to locate my new workplace at Tripler Army Medical Center, a massive brightly coral-colored building that sits on top of a hill and overlooks the valleys below. I smiled as I walked the halls of this huge facility, imagining what a wonderful, life-changing experience this would be for me and my wife.

My perspective of being on this beautiful, tropical island began changing as I continued having problems with my hiccups. My wife became more concerned and suggested I see a neurologist. So, I scheduled an appointment.

During the office visit, the neurologist said, "I'm concerned about your hiccups and the length of time you've been experiencing them." He looked down at his chart, then back at me and said, "I suspect you have a brain tumor. So, I'm going to order a magnetic resonance imaging, a MRI."

I didn't want to believe this news. It can't be, not me! Overall, I'm healthy. I take good care of my body. Maybe his diagnosis is not right, I thought.

I went in for the MRI, changed into a gown, and lay on the bed and was slowly transported into the big tunnel that awaited my presence. I was nervous laying in that hollow tube, listening to the pinging and hammering of that machine. Several times the technologist told me to hold my breath and not move. However, because I was so anxious, it was sometimes very difficult to do either of those requests. At times, my lungs felt as if they would burst from lack of oxygen. When I was finally given the okay to breathe, I desperately gasped for air. I took a long, slow breath in, and exhaled. I wondered, "*What are they seeing? Why is it taking so long?* Then, the tech announced I was done and thanked me for coming in.

A few days later, we received a call requesting that my wife and I come to the neurologist's office to discuss the results of MRI. I tried not to worry as I counted down the days to my appointment.

It was finally time to hear the results. We sat in his office, waiting anxiously for the doctor to finish his greetings and tell us what was going on. His expression became more serious, and he looked at us glumly and announced, "The MRI shows a massive tumor in the base of your brain, called Ependymoma, which is located in the lower back part of the brain called the posterior fossa. This type of tumor can block the flow of spinal fluid and put increased pressure on your brainstem, possibly causing you to experience difficulty walking, nausea, balance issues, vertigo, and other symptoms. So, we need to remove the tumor right away. We need to schedule you for an emergency surgery."

"What are the risk," my wife asked.

"The good news is that with this type of tumor, there is a 92 percent survival rate, depending on the patient's overall health. But, I won't lie to you," the doctor said, "There are some possible risks associated with surgery. Abraham may have a stroke, problems with speech or memory, lose strength in his legs or be paralyzed. He could also have a blood clot or swelling in the brain. He could even lose his life."

I sat there in shock, somewhat numb as I stared at the doctor in disbelief, not knowing what to say. I didn't know what I was going to be up against. But, I knew I had to deal with it.

When we left the doctor's office, the car ride home seemed longer than usual, and the quietness was almost unbearable. I could tell my wife was in deep thought. I was sure she was deeply concerned about me, and I wanted to remind her that I was in great shape. I am an athlete who works out every day and takes care of my body. She had enough on her plate, I didn't want her to worry.

Finally, she broke the silence, "Look! I'm shocked about all of this just like you are, and I'm scared at the same time, but we're not going to let fear dictate our lives. Remember, fear and faith cannot work together. The Lord tells us in Isaiah 41:10, 'Do not fear, for I am with you.' So we have to remind ourselves of ***His*** word, so we can't allow ourselves to give in to fear. And Abraham, remember 2 Timothy 1:7 clearly says, 'God has not given us a spirit of fear, but of power, love, and sound mind.' So, we have to trust and believe He'll see you through this. We're going to do whatever it takes to save your life. But above all, we're going to depend on God's word. I love you and I need you here with me, our family needs you. We are not going to even entertain the possibility of death—not at all. Do you hear me, Abe?"

"Yes," I said softly. "I will be fine," I said, trying to reassure myself.

"We serve a mighty God, and I know He will bring you through this. Just trust Him."

I smiled, knowing she was right, but doubt clouded my mind because I still wasn't sure why this happened to me. *God, why me?* I thought. *I am a tither and a man of God who loves you, and I am a covenant man who fears You.* I shook my head back and forth as if dislodging these thoughts. I had to get out of my head and help my wife plan a course of action.

So, we immediately gathered healing scriptures and God's promises and read them together. We listened to worship songs of healing, and we prayed. Then, we called our pastors, Art and Kuna Sepulveda, from the Word of Life Church in Hawaii, along with the other pastors, elders, and members of our church who know and believe that God can heal, and asked them to pray for my healing. Annette contacted family, friends, and people from our local church. Since she was planning to be with me at the hospital every day, she needed support. She also wanted her family who were stateside to come to Hawaii so they could help her with our three young children who were in elementary school. Her mother dropped everything and came to help us.

Four days later, I was checked into the hospital ready to undergo brain surgery with my wife by my side.

The surgeon came in and met with us briefly. "The surgery will be lengthy because of the complexity of removing the tumor from the base of your brain," he explained. "We expect the surgery to last approximately six to eight hours." Looking at my wife, he added, "So, I don't want you to be too concerned if Abraham is in surgery longer than that. This procedure takes time. I'll have someone give you updates from time-to-time, Mrs. Anderson. Any questions?"

"No!" we both said in unison.

"Just take care of my husband," Annette chimed, "and bring him back to me."

The doctor smiled, then nodded, "That's our goal," he said as he exited the room.

Surgery After Surgery

Surgery #1-Twelve hours later, I was still in the operating room. Hour after hour ticked by. Finally, after *eighteen hours* of surgery, the doctor informed my wife they had planned to remove all the tumor during the operation but, unfortunately, they were not able to. He said they would continue to monitor me in the hospital for a few days to a week or so. Then, I could go home and rest and come back in a month to have the remainder of the tumor removed. However, that didn't happen.

Eight hours later, my wife noticed the back of my neck was swollen like the size of an orange, and blood was visible inside the sac. She immediately buzzed for the nurse.

"Go get the surgeon," she demanded. "Something's wrong. The pig skin they used to cover his brain is filling with blood."

Surgery #2-The doctor examined me and said that my brain was hemorrhaging. They whisked me away to have an emergency surgery.

Annette didn't waste any time interceding on my behalf. She immediately went into prayer-warrior mode, believing God for a miracle. She asked the Lord to send ministering angels to surround and protect me. My wife continued to stand on God's word, no matter how gloomy the situation seemed. She was indeed my personal prayer warrior. Again, she contacted our pastors, and asked them to have our church members praying for my healing. They, in turn, assigned a pastor for support and encouragement to be with my wife daily. Annette also, contacted other churches and prayer centers to begin to pray for a miracle. The emergency surgery lasted for ten hours.

Surgery #3-We thought that after the second surgery I would be out of the woods. But believe it or not, a few days later, I had to undergo another emergency surgery because the bleeding in my brain had not stopped. During this emergency surgery, I coded once because of the brain hemorrhage. I had no heartbeat! But apparently, God wasn't ready for me yet, because the doctors reported that my heart started beating again on its own. I had to be placed on life support as an added precaution. This surgery lasted for eight hours.

The Final Surgery-I was scheduled for my final surgery to remove the remainder of the tumor. But after twelve hours in the operating room, the surgeon reported they could not get it all because my blood pressure kept going too high, and he didn't want to risk me having any further complications such as a stroke. *So a small portion of the tumor had to be left on my brain.*

After the multiple surgeries, my doctor recommended radiation therapy on my head to remove any other cancerous cells that may be lingering in my head. Before this could take place, I had to be fitted with a radiotherapy mesh mask that was molded to my face and secured to the table to ensure the radiation is targeted at the cancerous tumor during the radiation treatment. For six weeks, I underwent radiation, Monday through Friday for 30 minutes per session. This was exhausting.

During my stay in the hospital, my wife was my rock. She was very adamant about screening whoever requested to visit me. If their faith did not speak life and healing, they weren't allowed to see me. Her motto was, "No spectators allowed." This lady even refused to allow my Colonel and Sergeant Major to see me because she felt they didn't believe I could be healed.

At this point, I had been hospitalized for over a month. All of the surgeries and the radiation treatments were very taxing on my body. Being bedridden for this prolong length of time, caused my body to be extremely weak. This was a very trying time.

Meanwhile, the doctor felt my days on this earth were few, so he recommended that a priest come pray for me and administer my last rights. I thought I was going to die that day. I wasn't ready to leave my wife and family. At times, I felt helpless. Depression and anxiety crept into my mind. But even though I was in a physically weak state, I knew I needed to battle back spiritually. So I prayed the word of God over my situation, and with tears rolling down my eyes, I asked God to strengthen my body from my head to my toes. Then, I took a deep breath and exhaled and began speaking life over my body and recited Psalm 118:17 several times, "I shall live and not die. I *shall* live and not die."

Weeks later, I could feel the strength slowly coming back. I'm so glad I serve a God who answers prayers.

A Miracle Revealed

Approximately two weeks after my final surgery, the doctor said I needed to have one more MRI to see if the tumor had shrunk before I could be discharged from the hospital. The possibility of going home excited me.

Following the MRI, the doctor went to the waiting room to talk to my wife.

"Look, I can't explain to you what the MRI reveals. I think it'll be best if you come look at it yourself."

So Annette followed the doctor to the office and looked at the scans with him. He showed her the initial MRI which revealed the massive tumor. Next, he showed her the final MRI.

Looking bewildered, the doctor said, "We never mix theology and science, but I have to admit there was a supreme being over this case. I've never seen anything like it. We know for a fact that we left a portion of the tumor there, but look," he said, pointing at the scan, "it's completely gone!

There is *no sign of residual tissue from the tumor* in his head. *There's no sign of it at all!*" He said dismayed.

"It was nothing but God," my wife declared. "I told all of you from the beginning that God was going to remove my husband's tumor." Then, she looked up to heaven and whispered, "God, You *are* real!" she said, as a gentle smile spread across her face.

Through Sickness and Health, Our Marriage Commitment

When you are put in a situation where you are totally dependent upon your spouse, it makes you more grateful to have someone in your corner who can stand in the gap. My wife showed how much she loved me by putting everything on hold to take care of me from sunup to sundown.

During my darkest days and most challenging times, when I was unable to feed myself, my wife fed me breakfast, lunch, and dinner. She helped me to the bathroom each day and bathed me when the hospital nurses were busy or seemed overwhelmed. Annette walked with me, up and down the halls to help strengthen my legs. She pushed me in my wheelchair to ensure I got to my physical therapy sessions. At bedtime, my wife even got into bed with me and held me until visiting hours were over.

Throughout my stay in the hospital, my wife was always there to ensure everything went well. She even brought the kids to see me. That meant a lot to me, and it was good therapy for my soul. She told the nurses on each shift to play praise and worship music to ensure I kept my mind focused on healing. Through all of her actions during this trying time in my life, Annette demonstrated how much she treasured me and was committed to our wedding vows—for better or worse, in sickness or in health, so help me God.

When I think of how amazing my wife is, it brings tears to my eyes. I know that I'm a blessed man. All I have to do is look to Proverbs 18:22 in the New King James Version to confirm it. "He who finds a wife finds a good thing, and obtains favor from the Lord." A man cannot attain anything better than a good wife. With confidence, I can boldly say that my wife is a woman of valor who is strong and committed and is capable of accomplishing anything she puts her mind to. I believe she prayed me through the worst time of my life.

Finally Home

I was relieved when I was finally allowed to go home. When I was admitted to the hospital, I had no idea I would have to endure four surgeries and have to stay there for over a month. With everything I've been through and with almost losing my life, I wasn't sure if I would ever return to the place I call my sanctuary, my home.

As I entered the doorway, I was immediately calmed by the comfort it brought me. But then, my anxiety level began to overtake me. My heart was pounding fiercely against the walls of my chest, as questioning thoughts danced through my head. *Is my mind and body strong enough to do the things I need to do? Am I too weak to care for and protect my wife and family? Is my manhood going to be questioned? Can I fulfill my fatherly duties?* These thoughts were running wildly through my head. I decided to take these taunting thoughts captive by speaking God's words over my life, beginning with Philippians 4:13 which reminded me that "I can do all things through

Christ which strengthened me." This helped me to believe that I am capable of managing my daily responsibilities.

Conclusion

I don't have a secret potion that's responsible for restoring my health. My healing came through the Word of God, the Bible, filled with hope, faith, and God's promises. He is the main ingredient for my successful recovery. All the glory belongs to God!

Sometime later, I was able to return to my military unit, and by the grace of God, was able to complete all of my duties with no assistance. I passed my physical fitness tests with flying colors and met all my Army requirements. At my last duty site, San Diego Veterinary Command, I was eligible for promotion to Sergeant Major. However, that meant I would be transferred to the Sergeant Major academy in Fort Bliss, Texas, for a year or more.

But, after serving in the United States Army for over twenty-three years, I felt obligated to put in for retirement so Annette could complete her master's degree in nursing. She had sacrificed so much for me during my years of service to our country and during my extensive illness.

Some marriages may have been broken if they had to endure what we went through. But amazing as it is, this life-changing event strengthened our marriage. If it wasn't for my god-fearing wife standing diligently on the Word, I could have had a different outcome, and this season in my life may have been more challenging than it was. She was my voice when I could not speak, my legs when I couldn't walk, my mind when I couldn't express my thoughts. She was and is my everything!

Did you know God will place people around you in your time of need? He did that for us. We will be forever grateful to our family and friends who dedicated their time and effort in helping me heal and for being there to take care of our family.

I'm a living witness that if you put your faith in motion, God will perform miracles, if you only believe and trust in His Word. In Hebrews 10:23 of the Evangelical Heritage version, the Bible says, "Let us hold firmly to the confession of our hope without wavering, since He who promised is faithful."

I *am* a living miracle who can assure you of God's grace. My testimony of my battle with brain cancer and near-death experience is proof of God's merciful healing. I thank God for the opportunity to share my testimony. I pray He gives you the ear to hear and the heart to receive.

I will be forever thankful that the King (my God) in me transformed and healed the man I see in my mirror each day. MY GOD IS WORTHY OF ALL THE PRAISE, HONOR, AND GLORY. AMEN!

FRACTURED AND BROKEN

JEAN JOHNSON

The tapping on my car window woke me out of a peaceful sleep. All I could see was that big old hat that troopers love to wear.

"Sir," he said with a country drawl, "You can't be parked here like this."

I'm so grateful I'm a light sleeper. I rolled down my window and responded with a quick nod. "No problem, officer, I understand. Thank you." I started my car, and pulled off, driving with no destination in mind. I turned out of the parking lot and merged with traffic onto Broad River Road. *How did I get to this point in my life, right here*? I wondered.

There wasn't any traffic on the I-20 heading north to Allen University. I often parked there. Downtown Columbia, the inner city as they call it. In the cut. Real peaceful too. Peaceful, I repeat, because I know I have to get some more rest before I go to work. Yes, I had a job, a car, a wife, and a daughter. And if it wasn't obvious, a car that doubles as my home. Crazy, huh? Well, that's not the worst of it.

Marital Wilderness

How is that possible? Well, long story short, my wife and I were living in Atlanta. She was having a rough pregnancy, so wanted to move to South Carolina to be closer to her parents. And being the dude that I am and wanting to please her just like everybody else I've been around. I left my job of eight years at the university because I wanted her to have it easier. South Carolina, here we come. I've never had any problems getting a job. I have a job with the city of Columbia lined up for me, so I hit the SC working hard. I actually had two jobs. After all, I had a baby coming along. I was ready to do the daddy thing big time.

A few months later, my baby girl was born on September 11, 2000. We were so excited about her birth. I smiled as I watched her relatives surround my wife and our baby. I was glad we made the decision to come to South Carolina so she could have the support of her family and friends.

We struggled for the next two years. The incident that changed my mind about everything was when my wife went out one night and didn't come home until the next day. The problem with that was I was supposed to be at work at 5:00 in the morning. I had already used up all the excuses I could think of—my wife needed the car, my daughter was sick, the car wouldn't start, and so on. But this Sunday, I decided not to lie again. I did what I usually do. I couldn't hold it in any longer, I shed tears, manned up, and told my boss, Captain Hopkins, everything...leaving nothing out. Capt. Hop, as we affectionately called her, kept it real with me and told me the cold hard truth. It's better to have a job than none.

Capt. Hop was at my door in thirty minutes. My daughter was dressed and brought her to work with me. I was hella embarrassed. To my surprise, which I didn't initially see the blessing back then, but a few of the ladies at work had my back. They watched my daughter while I worked. I guess God knew my cup was as full as it could be that day. Emotionally, I couldn't even make it through the whole workday. I was a mess. Capt. Hop drove me to Ms. Elaine's where I picked up the baby and went home. She also arranged a few extra days off so I could work on my family issues. However, things didn't get any better.

My wife finally came home at 1:00 in the afternoon with her friends. I stood there watching as they laughed and joked with each other.

"Hey, we're going out to get something to eat," she said coyly. "I want to take the baby with me."

"That's fine, but we have to talk when you get back," I said, holding my tongue about my displeasure about her being out all night. Then, I watched her walk out the door without an apology or explanation.

Even then, I wanted to be a good man, a good husband, so I did what a good one would do. I thought I would relieve her of the tediousness of having to do her laundry so she wouldn't mess up her freshly done nails. I figured it would be like a peace offering. Well, a peace offering it was not. When I emptied her overnight bag, my heart sank. I stared in disbelief. I couldn't breathe. I was devastated. My innocent gesture turned out to be the mistake of all mistakes. I shook my head back and forth as I gasped for air. *How can this be?* I thought, looking at the proof right in front of me. She had been disloyal. What I saw actually killed me, my spirit, but yet it saved me, even though, at the time, it felt like a death sentence.

However, let me say this, I still refer to her as my wife, all the time. And in my heart of all hearts, I really, truly wanted her to stay my wife. I didn't want us to become a statistic, "another" failed black marriage. But the blatant disrespect she showed for our union, our promise, fractured our relationship.

All of these years later, I still don't take joy in airing out the details, but I will tell you that her infidelity broke me even more than I ever thought. I was battered and bruised with no self-love or concern for my own safety, welfare, or well-being, because who cares so little for themselves that they risk living in their car for months? Me. That's how I know I was broken—broken beyond compare. That is where the enemy wants you. And that's where I was stuck. So, I did what anyone would do. I dug deep into my past to figure out "what happened," "why it happened," and "how it happened" to help me understand how I got to be like I was. But as I looked back into my past, I realized that I was fractured way before my marriage. It actually started from my childhood.

Strong

Do you know these women—Mary, Ruth, Mary Magdalene, Rachel, Hannah, Deborah, Ester, Miriam, Sarah, Elizabeth, Priscilla, and Martha? They are from the Bible and are completely different from the women I grow up around, or should I say with. Ordinarily, I would say I wish I would have had one of them in my life instead of the ones I had, but that would be questioning God, wouldn't it? I believe so.

The ladies above were strong in their faith. Each and every one of these women had a love and admiration for the Lord, that is why I adored each of them. Their reverence for the Lord is greatly emphasized in the word. Testimonies of their deeds are gloriously preached, not only on Mother's Day, but every day! I can imagine the smile on your face now as you recited all of those names above, and I'm sure in the next passage, your smiles will be quickly wiped away. At the moment, I don't know if it will be of sadness or maybe even pity that you feel towards me for not having one of those loving, wholesome, and virtuous women in my young life. But the fact still remains they never existed in my world. And actually, I will go a little further and call it as it was for me. The traits of these Biblical women were not apparent in our house.

In my quest to get some understanding, I came across Hannah's story in 1 Samuel, Chapter one. Hannah was distraught because, despite all the things she did honorably before the Lord, she just couldn't have a baby. Her womb was closed, but yet day in and day out, and year after year, she continued to be faithful and giving. Time passed, and eventually, she was blessed with a baby. Samuel was his name. Even though she finally received the baby she had prayed for, she remembered her promise to give him to God, and she kept that promise. Because of her faithfulness, God blessed her with five more babies. Sometimes I wonder if my parents had known about some of these amazing women, would things have been different? Deep down inside, I wish I could have shared it with them.

But back to reality. Not in the Johnson's household. Although my mom and grandma seemed mad, angry, and hurt about something, I sure wasn't going to ask them any questions. Why not? Because they would have told me, "You're supposed to be seen and not heard." No, thank you. I avoided beatings as much as humanly possible. However, I can't truthfully say there were no feelings in our home. The typical emotions like caring, compassion, and tenderness, to name a few, did exist, and were expressed. But honestly speaking, it was few and far between. I even find it hard to explain this, and I don't actually feel comfortable calling it a feeling. It's more of a philosophy, a principal, or just the way the Johnsons were. Time and time again, it was said its "their way or the highway." You had to do everything according to the Johnson's rules. You could not have a difference of opinion. Does that make sense to you? Well, don't feel bad; it still doesn't make sense to me. In simple words, their way was just how it was, "Tough Love."

"Tough Love"

If you were to say apartment 9B had women who were loving, caring, nurturing, and supportive, people would think you were drinking something more than 100 proof alcohol, maybe even smoking something illegal, which was a possibility, if you were around our house too long. In all honesty, it hurts my soul to admit this, but the truth is the truth, and it will eventually set you free. There was no such thing in my life as a good wholesome loving woman. If you said, "The Johnson women were mean, ornery, spiteful, vindictive, and unremorseful parents," I would be like George Washington and repeat his most famous quote, "I cannot tell a lie." You are correct about that.

I can imagine the look on your face right now. If I were in your presence, you would be looking at me sideways, and maybe confused. The thought makes me laugh, because whenever I looked at my grandma sideways, she would say, "You looking at me like you want a beating." And like UPS, she aimed to deliver. Her first choice to use for discipline was Henry, a Weapon of Mass Destruction. And where I grew up, Henry had many siblings, and you had best believe if Henry came up missing, there was another one of his kin nearby known as an extension cord. And to add insult to injury, before swinging Henry in our direction, she always said, "This is gonna hurt me more than you." That was a bald-faced lie. Now, tell the truth and shame the devil. If that hurt our grandma or mom so much, why were we the only ones crying? I'm telling you the struggle was real in the Johnson house.

Another quote that became famous in our house was "spare the rod, spoil the child." And that was not happening in our house.

You don't have to be sad for me; I was sad for myself. There must be hundreds of questions on the tip of your tongue right now but hold your thoughts right now, because this is hard enough as is. I am placing my vulnerabilities out in the open to be viewed and judged, and that is the scariest of all realizations. Why? Because then I won't have plausible deniability. That's not only my shield but the shield of all men. Just deny it and fake it till you make it. And if you fake it long enough, you might believe it yourself.

"What kind of childhood did he have to totally slant his disdain for women?" you might ask. Well, it wasn't from other women at first; it came solely from my mother, because how many women did I know when I was just twenty months old? Go figure, right? It may be sad to say, but all I have are two memories of my mother. That's right, just TWO! Is that even possible? Yes, because they are exactly what they are, unresolved issues in my past, and they will remain that way until I resolve them or totally forget about them.

"Unresolved Memories"

When I think of these unresolved memories, I think of a song, "Afterwhile," by Kirk Franklin and Yolanda Adams that talks about pain going away after a while. However, my pain lingers on inside my soul. The scar is healed, but when I look inside, the ebb of the pain still throbs a little bit. When I'm in agony, I close my eyes and remind myself that it will be okay after a while, and I am grateful I have survived, unlike so many others who took another route. Thankfully, I didn't.

Psychiatrists believe it's possible to remember things that happened as a child. They believe some thoughts were buried deep inside in a place where you can actually forget them. That is until your defenses are down, and just like that, the wound is reopened, once again.

The first memory is when my youngest brother was four months old. My eldest brother and I were in the room just watching him. I walked over to the crib. Suddenly, my brother reached through the slats on the crib and bit my baby brother's hand. Needless to say, our mother rushed into the room, and guess who got in trouble because he was merely standing next to the crib? Yes, yours truly, me. Judgment was swift— she pushed me against the wall, and that's when I received my first taste of Johnson justice. Of course, more Johnson justice would be forthcoming. Do I have to say from who? I prefer not to, because the memories still make me look around fearfully as I did as a child.

The second memory was worse than the first. My baby brother was crying again, so this time, I went into my mother's room. I guess it was more pre-emptive action, so she couldn't or wouldn't blame me for his wailing. I saw her leaning against the bed. She didn't seem to notice that I had come into the room, so I walked around the bed to stand in front of her. I can remember seeing the tube tied tightly around her arm and the needle protruding out of it. As I gazed at my mother, dumbfounded, I didn't know what to think or what to do. I was just a kid. I called out to her, "Ma! Ma!" But my calls went unanswered—no response. Somewhere deep, down inside, I was strangely calm, because at that time, I didn't understand the finality of it all. After a few minutes, I went across the hall to the neighbor's house to get help, and that was it.

Throughout the years, I heard stories of how my grandma came to our house and threatened the staff from the Bureau of Child Welfare, Administration of Children's Services, the police, and anyone else she could curse out as she screamed, "Nobody's gonna get my damn grandkids!" Would you judge me harshly if I tell you that "had I known what I would have to endure in our household, I would have gone with the people from child services?"

I thought my mother was mean, but she didn't have anything on our grandmother, not Cora Mc Vincent—a pure Cherokee Indian born in 1910 in the Blackfoot hills in Roanoke, Virginia. She was proud of her heritage, but you can imagine how hard it was growing up in a family of eleven. Sometimes, you would hear her say, "You might as well buy your headstone if you come over to the Mc Vincent's house." It wasn't a threat; it was a promise. My grandma is a legend. Needless to say, I see where Johnson justice came from.

The first casualty of Cora Mc Vincent was my father, Lee Johnson. He might have been plenty of things, but he wasn't a fool. When I was about six years old, the whole neighborhood knew our father's whistle. As soon as he hit the block, we would hear it. We would look out the window to see where he was, but we knew enough not to mention it to our grandma. Do you want her to be mad? I think not. So, we would make excuses to go outside so we could meet up with him.

There were a few things my grandmother liked: 1) Cursing-She could curse better than any sailor. And believe me you didn't want any smoke from her, so of course, my father stayed clear of Ms. Mc Vincent. 2) The New York Mets-Kiner's Corner was her God. If you knew anything you would not trouble her during the broadcast of the game. 3) Drinking good old

Johnny Walker Black with Schaefer Beer. 4) Beating us—She was the sheriff, for sure. She would have the belt hanging over the door or a stick lying on the windowsill. Now, I know that's where my mother got it from.

One day, my grandmother said, "It's time to get in the shower."

So, all three of us boys quickly stripped our clothes off and jumped in the shower. We enjoyed playing in the shower, when suddenly the shower curtain was yanked back, and without a word, my grandma was swinging that belt, our skin stinging as the leather cut into our wet flesh. We were jumping around, screaming, and crying, trying to avoid each lick, shocked that she had caught us off guard again. This happened countless times, and I tell you nothing good came from that.

I know some people will think my grandma didn't love us, but I would disagree. But first, let me say one thing I learned from her is that a Johnson is going to defend a Johnson. That's my disclaimer. Does that mean I'm delusional or crazy? Maybe so; perhaps I have received too many hits. I know there is a word for it, Stockholm syndrome. Yes, that's it. I don't know if it applies to our situation, but in my heart I believe my grandma was mad, angry, or upset because she never truly dealt with the pain of losing her daughter.

I know you're wondering why my father was afraid of my grandmother, well here is the reason. One day our grandfather Odell came over, and he was a little tipsy. I never really knew why our grandfather wasn't home a lot, but I sure found out that evening. It was strange, to say the least, because that was actually the only moment I have ever seen a man come into our home. Our grandma didn't play that. I've heard her say plenty of times that her grandkids were her life now.

So, when Grandpa came into the house, and sat in grandma's recliner, we gasped and put our hands over our mouths, shocked because we all knew that was a no-no. You had to be bugging out to do that.

Our grandma, looking a little perturbed, said, "Boy, stop acting out."

But grandpa didn't stop. He laughed and grabbed her by the arm and pulled her onto his lap while we sat on the floor, curious about what would happen next.

"Don't you dare do that in front of the kids!" she said, irritated and pushed herself off of his lap. She stood up quickly and mumbled a few other words I'm not about to say here. Then, she stormed into the kitchen, and Grandpa followed close behind her, chuckling as he stumbled trying to maintain his balance in his tipsy state.

Being kids, we giggled a little as we made our way to peek into the kitchen. To our horror and regret, we saw him playfully spin our grandma around. It all happened so quickly. With a butcher knife in her hand, she sliced through the air—something dropped on the floor. Grandpa's eyes were huge with terror. He looked shocked as he cupped his hand against his face, blood streaming down like rain. Our mouths were wide open as we looked on the floor. She had cut off his ear!!! That was the last time I ever saw my grandpa.

Right then and there, I knew my grandma was not the one to mess with. I was an excellent kid from that point on, but that didn't stop the beatings we got because she believed in community punishment. If one child got in trouble, we all got in trouble. Or, as we would say, "All for one, and one for all."

I would have loved to say things got better, but they most definitely did not. They actually got worse. As a ten-year-old child, I was required to run errands that I should not have been allowed to do or go to places I shouldn't have been able to go. One incident that puzzles me even today occurred when I was just ten years old. When I got home from elementary school, my grandmother gave me a note to take to the package store on 116th Street and Lexington Avenue.

First of all, it was a mission requiring lots of maneuvering, because I had to navigate the streets that my eldest brother ruled. Avoiding him was always a task, only to be confronted by trying to cross Third avenue, which was like the New Jersey turnpike with lots of speeding cars. But needless to say, I did it because my grandma was more frightening than dealing with the traffic. That was just the start of it.

The next challenge was 115th street and Lexington Avenue. If you are from Harlem, you know about Lexington Avenue, Lean Central, the double H, Heroin Heaven. I would watch the drug addicts that hung around there and be amazed at how they would lean so low and still not fall over. I was sure none of them could catch me because I had experience running from my brother.

So, after I made it past those two obstacles, the package store was the easiest part. I hand-delivered the note and never looked in the bag that was given to me. Nope, I didn't look because I was sure my grandma would know, and as I said, I wasn't trying to get another beating. I was getting too old—I was almost eleven by that time.

As the years went by, I was still doing the same things. I must have been around fourteen years old by then when my grandma sent me to the package store again. I finally got the courage to look in the bag. It was a bottle of Johnny Walker Black and two cans of Red Devil Snuff. I can't really say I had an interest in it because we were always told to "stay in a kid's place." One Friday night, I decided to sneak the bottle out of the living room where my grandma had placed it and hide in the bathroom and take a taste. It was the nastiest thing I've ever tasted in my life, maybe with the exception of castor oil. It was really Nasty! That was the moment I believe I made up my mind never to drink in my life. And before you ask, I did get busted and got maybe my millionth beating.

Toward the end of the school year, I was so hyped that next year would be my senior year and maybe I could chill a little more. I thought with graduation coming up, I would be able to do so many things and explore adulthood more.

In June, after graduation, I came home expecting to be met with my grandma cursing me out, saying "Don't you know what time it is?" and so on. However, I was greeted with silence. Nothing!

"I'm gonna change clothes, and I'll be right back," I said. Still nothing at all, just silence. A few minutes later, I walked back into the living room, and there she was, sitting in her chair, her bag from the package store placed neatly on the windowsill, and her snuff on her lap.

My grandma was gone.

I felt like I was in a daze, a dream I couldn't wake up from as I walked through the house looking for my brother, calling his name. I checked the other two bedrooms, then, I realized he was not in the house. I looked out the window and saw him downstairs, sitting on the bench. I shouted down for him to come upstairs.

"What do you want?" was his reply. "You better not be wasting my time."

I walked away from the window and sat in the hallway, waiting for my brother to come up the elevator. It pinged, and he stepped out and walked toward me. I looked at him, scared, and not knowing what to say. I didn't know how to tell him what I had just seen because I was still trying to figure it out myself. Then, the first tear crept down my face. I couldn't hold them in anymore. The floodgate burst, and I cried as hard as I had ever cried in my life. I was all alone, truly alone.

My brother took a deep breath and walked into the house. All I could hear was him yelling and screaming, then silence, as he walked back out.

I was still sobbing uncontrollably as he walked past me. "Where are you going?"

"Back downstairs."

"Please don't leave me up here by myself with grandma. Stay up here with me, please," I begged.

He ignored my pleas, and I watched him walk slowly back to the elevator door.

He turned and looked at me, "Why should I? She only loved you, anyway," he sneered. And that was that.

It seemed as if I had waited for hours for help to come. Finally, the police came, and all they asked me was whether I had any adult relative or friend close by? I nodded, and went downstairs to Ms. Mamie's house, a friend of my grandma.

Ms. Mamie comforted me and told me that my grandma talked to her the other day about a dream where she was lying down and could see a bunch of flowers. She explained to me that Cora knew she was going to die, which made me feel worse. Ms. Mamie also told me that grandma knew it was time for her to go, but she didn't have to worry about me because I was going to be alright. She said she knew I would help look out for all of my siblings and that I shouldn't worry. It sounded okay, but I was still just seventeen years old going into my senior year of high school. I was in a daze until the funeral and during the rest of that summer.

The project manager for our apartment building, Mr. Robles, was a mean man. He didn't care about me losing my grandmother. All he said to me was, "How will *you* pay the rent?"

"I'll manage," I said. So, in my senior year. I made it work. Was it easy? Not for me. It's never easy for me. After school, I had football practice. Then, I would head to my new job at Key Food Supermarket stocking shelves and packing grocery bags. I did what I had to do to make things work to keep a roof over my head.

One day after work, I went home and found the door busted open, with no way to lock it. My brother was there with a house full of crackheads eating a dozen of my hard-earned eggs and a loaf of bread. That was the last straw.

Later that night, I pushed my bed against the door, so no one could get in. I picked up the only book my grandma had, the Bible. Reading the words from the Great Teacher, I found myself questioning God by asking, "Why does my life have to be this way?" and more "why" questions until I finally drifted off to sleep. Then, repeated the same actions the next day.

The next morning, my brother and his crackhead friends were still there as I maneuvered around them and out the door. I began doubting God even more. Where are your angels? I need help? I need a sense of hope.

"The Appointed Time"

Somehow, I felt in my heart that this day was different from any other day. Walking down the hall at school, I saw a dude named Darren Harris.

"Hi," he said as he handed me a flyer for Campus Life and invited me to attend a school Christian group meeting.

I agreed to go with him. What did I have to lose? I don't know why, but I poured out my soul to these people that I didn't know. I told them everything that was burdening me and every embarrassing thing about my life. To my surprise, there was no laughing, ridicule—nothing but all this God stuff. After the meeting, he came uptown with me and saw where and how I was living.

"Grab your stuff and come to my house," he said calmy.

"No," I said at first and made excuses because I was worried his mom would hear my story and say, "A Johnson kid! Nope, not in my house." But any place would be better than my current situation. So, I snatched up a few things, and we were back on the train heading out to Darren's house in Queensbridge.

Once we got to his house, I cried some more as I repeated my story to his mother, Jacqueline, or Jack as she is called. To my surprise, again, no judgment! She just hugged me. During my lifetime, I'm sure I have gotten hugs from my mom and grandma, but those were always after I got a beating. This was different. Even with a modest apartment with only three bedrooms for Jack, NayNay, Ty, Tyisha, Darren, Snook, and me, Jack made it work out.

Life was very different for me now. With every passing day, Queensbridge became more like my home. Over time, I met some more nice people in the neighborhood. Jack even told people that I was her other son. I was actually feeling like I belonged. In the process of getting used to my new family, I even gained a few aunts and an Uncle Moe.

Psalms 94:14 in the New Living Translation says, "The LORD will not reject his people; **he will not abandon his special possession**." With all that I have been through in the past, and even though the future might bring more issues, this is one verse that has kept me and will continue to hold me steadfast throughout it all.

It is so easy to just give in when you're bombarded with life's challenges. Way too easy. The enemy wants you to feel that way, just like Adam and Eve. They were so ashamed, they preferred to hide themselves instead of bowing down and asking for forgiveness. God is a Loving God. So loving, he gave His only Son, Jesus Christ, to cover us. So, ask yourself, how could someone give so freely to pay for the sins of the world, to make a way for us to receive all that is promised to us?

Beware! The devil wants us at the point where we are so deep in despair that we don't believe anyone, not even God, could love us that much. But all you need is just a mustard seed of faith and accept the God-fearing people God has placed alongside you to encourage you to carry on. Believe me, I know for a fact that even though you can be "Fractured and Broken" into many pieces, He can put you back together. Together, better than ever. So just hang in there and believe.

Despite all I have gone through, I am here now. My heart could have been dark as Job's wife's to where I would speak nothing but curses because of what all has happened to me. But I smile, I laugh, I love, and most of all, I have hope that everyone can feel the peace I feel, in spite of their past. God kept me, like I know he can and will keep you. No matter what you face in life, just trust Him, and never give up.

SECOND CHANCES

CHRISTOPHER LEONARD

For many years, I perceived myself as a mistake. A mistake is defined as "an action or judgment that is misguided or wrong." Truthfully, when you make so many mistakes, you begin to view yourself as such, stripping your identity and not giving change the opportunity it deserves.

I grew up different; I never hung around kids my age. The people I saw as associates or friends were hustlers, robbers, pimps, con artists, etc. It was through them that I was exposed to what life had to offer. It wasn't until years later I realize this was just one side of the coin. See, when you choose to view yourself as a mistake, you begin to accept certain environments as normal, but you must realize that you can learn from those people and decide to be different.

There's value on both sides of the coin—good value and bad value! But it is how you view them both that will determine your fate! It's hard to recall the night that changed my life because it was an ugly and costly version of myself. This night would have me questioning my very existence in this world, hearing my heartbeat so rapidly while an inner voice was saying, "How the fuck did I end up here?"

One night, it was me and the former love of my life showcasing ourselves in the worst manner, with no concerns of how we should stop things from going too far, or better yet, saying, "It's too late!" As the reader, you are probably wondering, what night I am talking about. The night I was charged and arrested for a crime I did not commit, "First Degree Rape! On top of that, they added Domestic Violence, Second Degree!"

With such a falsehood and horrendous narrative hanging over my head, I didn't know what to think or do. I just prayed and hoped not to kill myself over a lie.

But before I dig too deep into my story, I must shine a light on my "early years" when I was just a sophomore in high school. Remember, there are two sides to every coin. If my coin had the words, fear and faith, on each side, where would mine land? On fear? On faith?

For many years I was known to my family as the prodigal son. The one who made many mistakes, bad decisions, lacked accountability, but, most importantly, self-worth. I deceived myself into believing that I was not worthy enough to change! I was foolishly wrong! It wasn't until I truly bumped my head with my first real love, "basketball," that I lost myself. After getting kicked off the team towards the end of my junior year in high school, I began smoking weed, heavily, to try and find my self-worth!

It was the spring of 2002, and basketball season had just wrapped up. I was undecided if I wanted to go forward and play on the varsity team because my Junior Varsity coach had told me he wouldn't be coaching anymore. He didn't understand that it was his focus and efforts the impressed upon me that helped me get better with each game. And now he's quitting because the school offered him a chance to be a principal or assistant principal.

Later, I realized that although I would be losing him on the court, I would be gaining an advocate and ally in the school hallways. So, I kept playing ball. My dad had always raised me with the saying, "Leonard's don't quit; we just keep building 'til we win!" So that was what I set my mind on doing!

Around this time, my father and I had begun to become closer and actually have a solid relationship. I wasn't afraid nor ashamed to tell him things that were on my mind. But on this particular spring day, my whole attitude changed drastically. It was a Thursday evening; I had just gotten out of spring practice and had made it home and the house phone rang!

"Hello!"

"What's up, son?" my dad said. "I need to talk to you about something; you are not in trouble, but it's important that we talk. I'll be there in a few minutes."

"Okay," I said reluctantly.

When dad got home, he told me to follow him into his office. "Have a seat," he said with a serious look on his face. "Son, I have to deploy to Afghanistan for a while, and I don't know when I'm coming back."

I looked at him, shocked. I couldn't help it, but I immediately broke down and started crying, "Why do *you* have to go? Why can't someone else go?" This was some of the most hurtful news of my life, my dad's going to be re-assigned to Afghanistan. *What am I supposed to do?* I thought. This is the end of my sophomore year of high school, I need him around to help get me through my junior year.

"Son, this is what I signed up for," he said, shaking his head. "Life isn't fair, but this is something I must do!"

I couldn't stop the tears, I tried, but they kept flowing down my face. What am I going to do without my dad?

My father, sensing my anguish and pain, reached out and hugged me. For the first time in a long time, my father held me like I was a little kid.

"Everything is going to be alright. But I need you to behave and do right by your mother and sister."

I nodded, assuring my dad that I would be the man of the house while he was away. Unbeknownst to me, this would mark the beginning of a pattern of changes that I couldn't control, doors opening that I couldn't close willingly, and trouble impacting me that only faith and God's will could deliver me from. This was a moment in my life that I like to label as "Lost."

Lost would become a common word for me towards the last couple of years of high school. Now, with my father gone to fight in the war and me living in Alabama with my mom, I was once again stuck with a road map that would be hard for me to interpret. Especially, when my feelings toward my existence had become so numb. But that's when God began to push me forward, kindling relationships with certain people.

My brother, Christopher Demond Carter, was a true character! He didn't give a damn about what he said and how he said it, even more so, he did it all with a smile on his face! It was his soul and character that helped me navigate through life's most challenging moments. He gave me the greatest gift one man could give to another, "belief!"

I became lost, not knowing my purpose. The only thing I was good at was getting into trouble and debating my way out of it! My first steps into my junior year of high school were so essential—steps into a new beginning, ones that would be costly but well worth the lessons given. See, when you get older, it's not about your age changing; rather, it's more about your perception.

Independent Thinker! When you think about being an independent thinker, who would you be? What would you look like? Would you become perfectly made? HELL NO! A great independent thinker must fail in the worst way and have their sights and/or insights tested! Sometimes that requires you to hang around people who do not have your best interests in mind, forcing you to fight for your best interests while learning the true value of partnership!

My junior year was preparing me for the fight of my life—rejection, disappointment, financial woes, and mainly, uncertainty! I didn't know who I was. I just knew I didn't fit in. I thought me and my best friend, David Sapp, were going to have some of the best times of our lives. It was his senior year, and you know that means parties, late nights after rivalry games, and driving around smoking blunts, better known as "blunt routes." Oh, plenty of the finest pine was being smoked day and night, from morning to the last call for alcohol!

Most importantly, it would be my first year playing varsity basketball—a dream short-lived due to my attitude and lack of accountability. As a consequence of my own actions, I realized I had to find purpose and passion via other means. Through David Sapp's father, Mr. George Sapp, I found a man that helped mentor me along my journey to become a man, holding me accountable for my foolish decisions and forcing me to become more responsible and aware that my life matters! It was cool hanging with Mr. Sapp. He has a way of convincing you to challenge what you see in yourself, compelling you to become an independent thinker!

What I love about him is his transparency, sharing his story and how he fought to change himself for his family and society. He's been sober for multiple decades now! He was the first person that I could remember to ask me, "What do you want to be when you grow up?" When he asked that question, he genuinely wanted to know my response!

The purpose of my story is to show you how transitions in life can be a mother fucker! It takes a lot of grit and will to see that your next decisions are the ones that make the challenges that will define and refine you.

It was the fall of 2003, a year when I found how unpopular and unpredictable the truth could be! Around this time, life was showing me how foolish I had been and how I had become dependent on marijuana to cope with the demands and rejections I experienced. I was going to school high almost every day, not focused, and always in trouble. This is not the model behavior for a high school athlete!

I thought I was hiding my patterns well, but I wasn't. My coaches, teachers, and friends all knew that I wasn't myself! I had allowed life's challenges to convince me of a false reality. For instance, the first three months of my junior year, I was in and out of the principal's office, mainly because I didn't respect authority or value rules. I believe this was because my father had gone to fight in the war, and wasn't there to guide or discipline me, so I could care less about what any teacher or principal had to say.

It wasn't until I struck a nerve with the assistant principal that I was smacked with reality! I got in trouble in English class and was sent to the principal's office for talking back. When I walked into the principal's office, Coach T was there, I knew this wasn't going to go well.

"Leonard, you're suspended indefinitely from the basketball team, but you're still required to be at practice every day and still have to complete your required conditioning drills."

This verdict truly sucked but kept me humble. Later, I learned that this was psychological warfare! I thought that fights were only physical and not mental. I was so far from the truth. The greatest fights were fought by penmanship and mental warfare. See, the principals, teachers, and coaches had it figured out, if I beat you up mentally, your physical behavior will self-destruct!

So, I stayed humble while walking around on eggs shells. The teachers and authority figures knew about my indefinite suspension from the team and were waiting for me to slip-up so they could see me get kicked off the team for good. I refused for as long as I could to not fall victim to their preying behavior. I made it through temporarily and was afforded the opportunity to be back on the team, just not varsity!

This was when the psychological warfare ignited at an all-time high. Coach T told me that I would have to prove myself by playing on the Junior Varsity team and keep my nose clean. I mean the nerve of this dude, playing along with their pursuit to belittle and trigger me to react out of control. But I didn't take the bait. I kept a level head as best as I could, but it wasn't enough. After the season ended, I did my best to focus on the future.

Unfortunately, I slipped up and got in trouble in history class for chewing gum and being irritated when told to spit it out! My history teacher was a non-black football coach, and I believe he was upset because he and his coaching staff were being fired for the awful seasons they had. Additionally, he and I used to joke with each other quite often, but I had a way of making everyone in the class laugh. Truthfully, they were probably all laughing at me rather than with me. One day, I apparently made him so mad that he walked me to the coaches' and principal's office, demanding that I be removed from his class, stating that I was distracting the other students from learning! The lies adults told just to cover up their own pride and feelings!

So, later that day, I was called into Coach T's office. He looked at me, disappointment showed across his face. "Sorry, Chris, but you're kicked off the team, but this time, for good!

I had never been so upset, truly furious, and frustrated. Tears streamed down my face and anger pulsed through my veins, along with a crushing feeling of disappointment in my heart!

"This is bullshit!" I yelled, glaring into his eyes. "I didn't do anything! The teacher is holding a grudge against me."

"I don't care, Chris! You were warned and you were given a second chance. You blew it."

Honestly, I was highly pissed with him because that son of bitch made me sit through an entire practice just to tell me afterward that I was kicked off the team! He knew all along that his mind was already made up. Hell, I could have been at home getting high, eating a pizza, doing anything other than wasting my time here! No worries, I have plenty of time to do it now! I seemed to have lost my edge, focus, and faith!

All I wanted to do was play on the same team as my close friend, Bull. See, back then, Bull was the truth in basketball, establishing himself as a phenomenal athlete with the capacity to change the narrative of any game. Together, we played our very best because I knew my role, and he knew his, and we never crossed over into each other's lane.

My life was wounded and damaged by what I thought would be my future. But, thankfully, I had people in my corner who wouldn't give up on me. Mr. Sapp, his son David, and my friends, Ray and Chris, kept me grounded and standing. Mr. Sapp and David gave me a chance to grow and learn principles for building community and brotherly fellowship. Mr. Sapp also emphasized the concept, "You can do anything you want, but you must build a support system for it." David showed me how to keep a level head and give myself a chance to be successful.

Whereas Ray and Chris's approach was very different. They taught me to fight and stand up for myself, to never back down from any fight, and to just keep fighting regardless of the outcome. Their motto was "*Life, at times, is about fighting, not winning. Once you learn how to give the first punch, then you can improve your technique for winning.*" They encouraged me even more by saying, "Remember, every man falls; it is his efforts to get up that will determine how he stands!" I was determined to try and live by everything my friends had taught me.

At the end of my junior year, I had just finished all my exams and was merely at school, just killing time. I saw David in the hallway, and he was preparing to leave, so I figured I would leave with him. Everything was going smoothly. We were moments away from leaving until one of the assistant principals saw me and made it his priority to stop me.

"Leonard, where are you going? he asked.

"Home, I'm finished for the day," I said.

"No, I don't think so," he said, as he attempted to stop me. "You'd better not leave. I'm warning you! You don't want to do this."

"Watch me," I retorted, refusing to listen to anything else he had to say. I left on my own terms. I didn't realize this spur-of the-minute decision would come back to bite me later.

Prior to the start of my senior year, I had to meet with the Superintendent of County Schools. I sat across from him as he drummed his fingers on his massive desk while looking intently at me.

"Leonard, do you recall that incident with the assistant principal at the end of your junior year? You were disrespectful and you didn't follow his instructions. He told you that you couldn't leave, but you left anyway. We're not going to tolerate any more of this insolent behavior from you! It is not acceptable! So, this is the ultimatum, if you have one more incident at that school, you're going to be put out for good! Do you hear me—for good? You will be expelled! We're not going to tolerate disrespectful behavior from you or anyone else.

Well, it didn't take long. It wasn't even two months into my senior year when another incident occurred. Me and a guy who I've known since grade school got into it about something stupid, a female. The silly thing is that neither one of us was dating her—it was just fuel to start a fire!

This fire was the one that got me suspended from school, and I had to go live with my dad. See my mom and I had made an agreement that if I got in trouble one more time, I would have to go live with him. Fortunately, he had just come back from the war, so it was perfect timing for me to go live with him. After I got settled in, he enrolled me into Grissom High School, a predominantly white school that wasn't too fond of black people being there.

I didn't want to go Grissom, but because I refused to follow the rules at my previous school, I had no other choice! So, I went to school every day and stayed to myself. I figured this way, no one could get me in trouble but me!

My father had tried multiple times to contact the coach, but to no avail. I was determined to get on the team. So, I went to see Grissom's head basketball coach and asked if I could try out for the team. He told me that he would have to discuss my request with his staff and would let me know his decision.

A few days had passed when his assistant coach saw me walking in the hallway and called my name. He requested that I follow him into the head coach's office. The coach beckoned for me to come in and sit down. He wasted no time and told me he had talked to my former coach, who said I was a good kid with potential, but that I smoked weed and hung around the wrong people. He asked me if there was any truth to what my former coached said.

At first, I was going to lie, but something came over me, and I admitted that it was true. Unknowingly, my telling the truth would afford me the opportunity to play basketball one more time. The coach told me he respected me for telling him the truth and that I would have to stay clean and pass random drug tests. I agreed and felt hope come alive inside me, once again. I thought, *second chances really do exist*!

In three months, my attitude, focus, and efforts toward success began to have a pace to it, one that I had a chance to control. For the first time, I experienced humility in a way that made sense. It was like I truly had a fresh start, an opportunity to stretch myself on a different level by letting uncertainty be my guide.

Stupidly, I inevitably took this gift for granted, letting comfortability settle in on me! I forgot my goal— mind your own business and stay in your lane! It was 2004, homecoming weekend. We had just finished our early morning workouts and were taking team pictures. While I was walking down the hallway at school when I and ran into some of the guys I spoke to at times. They told me about these white guys that took sheets and made Klu Klux Klan masks and wore them to school for homecoming. Furthermore, they said they weren't required to take them off until the end of the day. I was highly pissed and asked them what they were willing to do about it. Before I finished my sentence, the white brothers were walking through the entrance into the hallways.

Immediately, I approached them and said, "Hey, you think wearing a Ku Klux Klan mask to school is funny?" Then the oldest brother intervened, and we began to exchange words. Hearing the commotion, some teachers ran down the hallway to break us up. That's when I scattered and ran to class. I dropped my books off in my science class and was getting settled in when I saw a friend of mine going up the hallway. I eased out of my seat to go catch up with him. When I opened the hallway door, I ran into the brothers, and that's when our words turned into action. Everything happened so quick! I got jumped by the brothers, but only me and the oldest brother got in trouble and were kicked out of school. We were both forced to finish our senior year at an alternative school.

My second chance was gone, with no hope of return, all because I didn't mind my business and stay in my lane. My family and others viewed my circumstances as unruly and racist. After seeking legal advice from the NAACP, we sought advice from an attorney they recommended in Birmingham and began to appeal the school's decision. This process went on for roughly ten months, only to receive the same verdict, expelled from school!

Eventually, I graduated in the spring of 2005 and began working as a land surveyor. I thought this was going to be my job for the rest of my life. My parents had a different plan. They were applying to colleges daily so I could go to school. I couldn't believe it, but I was accepted into Stillman College, an Historic Black College University (HBCU) located in Tuscaloosa, AL. I didn't want to go there, but my parents only gave me three options, school, military, or live on the streets. I reluctantly chose the streets initially because I didn't think I was good enough for college and that I wouldn't fit in.

It wasn't until I spoke to my grandma and my friend, Pooh, that I was convinced to give college a chance. They both told me that I should do it for at least a year and see what I could learn. So, I agreed, it was the least I could do for my grandma; she had always been there for me and supported me unconditionally.

College! The American dream where kids fresh out of high school can go and learn how to be successful and take care of their families! I would later learn that this was all a lie! College is nothing but a place to accumulate massive debt and possibly obtain a useless degree. For me, it was a place where I got a chance to meet my brother from another mother, "Jeremy Managen!" At first, Jeremy and I didn't like each other. It wasn't until a year later that we actually understood that we needed each other, and both had the same interest—to become successful.

My first year of college was rough! I didn't really have any friends, all my classes started early in the morning, and I didn't have a car! It wasn't until the spring semester that I met a professor by the name of Dr. Love, who would convince me to see myself differently, challenging me to pursue options for my life. She was the one professor who convinced me to stay in school.

College was the place where I met the woman who I considered to be the "love of my life." Why? Because physically, she checked all my boxes: fine as hell, with a phat ass, nice chest, pretty face, and the influence to make me feel like a man, her man! Later I would learn that I was loyal to a fault with her, normalizing dysfunction. Most importantly, I would learn that I let her words have too much influence over my feelings. Such actions would cost me deeply, losing my freedom and sense of self-control. As a man, you must understand not to let anyone, especially a woman, dictate your behavior and how you respond to situations.

In January 2011, my relationship with Lady X took a turn for the worse. All the lying, cheating, and dysfunction finally led to a night that I would resent living. It was the weekend of January 9, 2011, Alabama had won their first title with Nick Saban, and Tuscaloosa was on fire! There were parties everywhere with all the vices that you could enjoy. My neighbor asked me to take his cousin out on the town and show him around, so I did just that. Amid that, Lady X called and asked me to come over after the celebration, and I agreed.

I showed up at Lady X's house before 3:00 am, but she wasn't happy. We began to argue but eventually settled down after she ate the food I had brought her. Afterward, we became intimate, fulfilling each other sexually, until it happened, "whiskey dick," I couldn't get an erection! I learned then that Makers Martin bourbon and I were not meant to be friends.

That's when her mind began to speculate, accusing me of messing with the same woman she had caught me cheating with days before. Suddenly, our relationship changed drastically. We were fussing and fighting like cats and dogs. Before long, the police had come and kicked the door down, placed me in handcuffs, drove me downtown, and booked me.

I panicked when I realized where I was! "Why am I being booked in the homicide unit instead of the city jail?" I asked the officer.

"They'll explain everything to you when you get there," he responded.

They put me in a room like I was on the TV show, the First 48. I wasn't sure what was going on. I was anxious and shivering from the cold that permeated my body. They made me wait for hours before anyone came in to talk to me.

Finally, the detective came back in, sat across from me. He glared at me for a moment before asking, "So, what happened?"

I explained exactly what had happened. "My girl was mad because I had gotten to her house so late. But after talking, she calmed down and we started making out. Then, things took a turn for the worse when I couldn't get an erection during our sexual intercourse. She started jumping to conclusions about things, and after yelling back and forth, we began brawling with one another.

Apparently, he didn't believe me because this same detective made me strip naked and took pictures of my private parts. Then, he looked at me and said I was being charged.

I asked, "What am I being charged with?"

"Domestic Violence, for now."

But later, he came back and said something I will never forget.

"You're being officially charged with First Degree Rape and Domestic Violence Second Degree," he announced smugly.

My heart sank, and it was hard to breathe as I heard him say the word, "rape" because I knew that he was lying and putting false charges on me with no evidence. They took me to jail, and I was able to post bond. I was released late that Sunday evening. I took these circumstances hard because I wasn't sure how this was going to impact my life because of the lie that was being told and portrayed by the detective.

One night, it was late, and I was struggling with my thoughts. I called my brother and said, "Chris, I'm contemplating suicide. I am willing to end it all right now!"

"No!" he immediately cried out. "You and I both know you didn't do this! You doing that would not only kill you, but it would kill me too!" For the next few moments, he tried to encourage me by saying, "I need you to stay focused! Don't give up! Everything will work out. Man, you got to trust God!"

To hear him say "trust God," was really huge because he wasn't the religious God-fearing type, so that let me know that God was using him to get to me. Days later, I received a call from my attorney to come see him at his office, and I did. I explained to him what happened that night, and he immediately started taking notes and began processing everything. Once I finished, he called the district attorney and lead detective's office, asking them what evidence they had and how strong their case was.

The detective explained, "We don't have him on the rape charge, we just charged him with it because we knew we could, but he's definitely going down for the domestic violence for sure!"

Again, my heart dropped! I couldn't believe how corrupt these people were. My lawyer found out they had revoked my bond, so that meant I needed to turn myself in so I could have control over the situation.

Jail is a place where no man should pursue being. This is a place where men are treated less than human beings. They are considered property, county and/or state property. Being in jail taught me how to appreciate the small things, respect, manners, and the importance of reading books. My first six months in jail, I was in a dorm with no TV; the only thing that I had to entertain me was the Bible and my books. So, I began reading the Bible, mainly Acts, Romans, and First and Second Corinthians. The first book I read was called the Disclosure. It was a great read that opened my mind up to a new reality, one that wasn't conformed to the content on TV.

Being in jail taught me how you must have a focus for fighting, mentally and physically. You have to learn how to trust the will inside of you, to become your own advocate, and not to take any shit off anyone, even yourself. Most importantly, don't let your emotions or feelings lie to you. The moment you show weakness when you're behind bars, is when the wolves come out, looking and smelling blood to feast on! It's all about mental warfare, doing more listening and less speaking.

Within six months of being incarcerated, I had my preliminary hearing. During the proceeding, the state was required to present all the evidence they had against me. However, throughout the process, the state never presented any form of actual evidence. They only provided "hearsay" testimony. The strongest leverage they had was utilizing Lady X on the stand in hopes of winning the judge over with her tears and display of emotions.

I must admit, seeing her take the stand against me shattered me to the core. It showed me how real my circumstances were. With only hearsay evidence presented in court, my lawyer and I figured the case would be dismissed or at least, I would get my bond reinstated once they presented the results from forensics. I felt confident as I waited for the judge to grant me bail.

My hopes were quickly dashed when the detective and district attorney made their announcement to the court, "Your Honor, the forensics results have not been processed yet."

Immediately, I knew that meant more time in jail for me until the trial. It took eighteen months, but I was finally headed to trial. I didn't know what to expect or how things were going to go. Then right before the trial started, my lawyer pulled me aside and explained that he and the district attorney had reached a plea deal, which required me to do five more months and plea out to the following: Domestic Violence 2nd degree, Possession of Marijuana 1st degree, and misdemeanor of Sexual Misconduct.

Finally, on December 10, 2011, I was released from jail. I had spent twenty-three months away from the world, and for eighteen months, I didn't know when or how I was coming home. I just had to trust God's power and pray. But thankfully, I made it through! Getting released taught me the power of survival and how mental toughness is key to overcoming any challenge!

My first year out was tough! I was dealing with depression and anxiety while fighting to finish college. At the same time, I was preparing to have my first kid. So, I leaned on my mentor Mr. Sapp and my dad to help me. My dad had done some research on a school called Athens State University (ASU). One of their business programs taught great techniques for their students to excel in corporate America. I enrolled there and was accepted. I was hell-bent on being successful. I wasn't going to let the events of my life determine my future.

During the winter of 2014, I graduated from ASU with a bachelor's degree in Business Management and a Minor in Marketing, along with certifications in Enterprise Resource Planning (ERP) and Software Applications Products (SAP). Years later, I went back to school and received my master's degree in Management from the Florida Institute of Technology in the fall of 2017.

Mr. Sapp helped me get enrolled in Vocational Rehabilitation Services. This organization helped me find gainful employment and a great therapist who helped me navigate through my mental woes. While going through the program, I learned that everything you do is predicated on your mental awareness as well as your comprehension skills. This process required a lot of patience and faith, and with the hope that my efforts would prepare a better future for me.

Eventually, after all the hard work from school and consistent employment, I was afforded an internship in the defense industry for contracts and acquisitions. This opportunity was fruitful for me. It taught me how to manage myself in certain environments while learning how to take my thoughts and make them plans of actions.

Fatherhood! It was a blessing in disguise! It made me start looking at the big picture, becoming selfless and determined to give my firstborn son a future that wasn't predicated on his father's mistakes. Through it all, I was just grateful that God always kept me gainfully employed and provided opportunities for me to meet people that would help shape my future. Years later, I had a second son in 2016. I was blessed to obtain full custody of both of them by 2021.

Honestly, I did not recognize the King in me until I lost three of the most significant people in my life! On September 17, 2017, my best friend and brother, Christopher Demond Carter, was killed. The pain I felt from his death was indescribable, but his funeral reminded me how many people's lives were impacted by him and the mark he left on the world.

In September 2020, I lost the greatest cheerleader and supporter I've ever had, my grandmother, who died from conditions that were beyond our control.

Lastly, in November 2021, my long-time best friend, Jeremy Managen, was killed in the most devasting way. His presence, just like my brother's, had a great effect on his community and the people connected beyond it.

The deaths of these three people changed my life in a major way. It has made me fight to live life to its fullest and die empty. I owe it not just to myself, but to those who made it possible for me to be where I am today.

Most importantly, it showed me that you must have a heart for yourself. You must fight for your confidence and not listen to the negative rhetoric that people say about you. The challenging question is, "What do *you* say about yourself?" Many people will say, "Enjoy the journey," but I say prepare for it and step forward into uncertainty, and don't stop swinging and moving forward until you get to the other side. Remember, there are always two sides to a coin, so flip it to see if you will land on Heads or Tails!

My journey begs to ask the question: "When did you see the Man in the Mirror?" Honestly, I'm telling you my story so that I can keep my past in the past, and not allow it to interfere with my present anymore, or my future. See, it's about knowing when to end a chapter in your life, period. We must remember that no matter what events occur in our lives, they're just like chapters in a book. Although it may be terrifying, at times, you can close that chapter and move on!

While writing this chapter, I felt nervous, scared, vulnerable, and anxious because I realize that by writing this chapter, my life is no longer my own. It's tough because I never wanted to put so much of myself on public display, but that's how I know there's absolute value here. I know that if I do this now, I can break the chains that once held me down!

It's either "Get Rich or Die Trying," wise words from the legend himself, "50 Cent." When I look at the first part of the phrase, "Get Rich," it reminds us that if you face your fears with no remorse, just endless efforts, you become enriched, and your faith is strengthened because your fears do not keep you bond. The phrase, "Die Trying," means you are fighting to die empty, leaving everything you have on earth, and looking back with no regrets, just lessons learned. But you should also leave behind clues to success for others to follow and build upon There is healing in putting your testimony out there because it can help someone else in their struggles. That's why I am so appreciative that the King in me has transformed the man I see and put it on my heart to write my story!

Finally, I just want to give this life all I've got until someone, God, cuts the lights off on this small planet!

FATHER BY BLOOD BUT NOT BY BOND

JABARRIE MONSANO

My story is not your typical story. Rather, it is a blueprint for many others who may have gone through a similar journey as I did. I am sharing my life experiences in hope of empowering others to courageously navigate their own pathway. You see, my father has never played a significant role in my life. There has never been a moment that I can recall that was memorable enough for me to describe his involvement as "prominent" or "influential."

When I was growing up, I didn't realize that I did not have a father or significant father figure in my life. It wasn't until I was six or seven years old that I became aware of the glaring reality of my circumstances. It occurred when many of my elementary school friends were speaking about their dads and how much they did for them.

Eventually, when it was my turn to enter the conversation, I simply had one response, "I actually don't know my dad."

Naturally, my friends were shocked and started asking questions or making comments like, "What happened?" "No way!" "Really?" "I'm sorry." "I feel bad for you." These were just some of the many responses I received.

Now, a lot of people may look at me not having a father in my life and point out the disadvantages that are associated with it and naturally expect me to react negatively towards it. However, I never thought about not having a father as a bad thing because I was surrounded by aunts, uncles, cousins, grandparents, and of course, my mother, who all supported and guided me through life.

As a kid, when I heard that my father was coming to see me I remember being very excited. I would jump for joy and always had a smile on my face while rushing around to pack my bag so I could spend time with my dad. But after hours upon hours of anxiously waiting for him to arrive, I was devastated when he *never* showed up. I did not understand why my father would say he was coming, and then not show up. Didn't he know I wanted to see him, to have father-son talks with him, and to just spend time with him? The rejection was crushing.

My mother could always sense my pain and disappointment. In an attempt to make me feel better, she would always come up with excuses. "He probably got caught up at work. Maybe he's tired. He's probably stuck in traffic," and the list goes on.

Of course, as a kid, I believed these excuses and did not really question them. This was true for me until these excuses were so drawn out and repetitive that they transitioned from excuses to the expected responses to my dad's disappointing no-shows. The change in expectation shifted my outlook on what my father meant to me.

Around the age of ten, I started asking my family members questions about my father, attempting to get a better understanding of why he was not present in my life and if there was any specific reason for his absence. To my surprise, there was not a single relative that could give me a definitive answer why my father behaved like this. They all remember him being caring, protective, and intelligent. Even my mother told me that she thought my father was going to be the best dad. She said, when they were together, she would not have chosen anyone else to have a child with other than my father.

Taking this information in was confusing. For my dad to go from what people described as an amazing person as a young adult to an absentee father who was non-existent in his son's life and who didn't seem to care about his own child. This was something that my whole family was not expecting. However, it was the reality they had to come to terms with, and eventually, so did I.

The moment I came to understand how I felt about my father was when I had to make a decision of either going to spend the day with him or sleeping over at my cousin's house. The moments of past disappointments had truly settled in my mind, and without a moment of hesitation, I chose sleeping over at my cousin's house over spending some quality time with my father. I was over the false promises and excuses and realized that my father wasn't giving me the time of day. So, why should I give him something he's not giving me?

At this point in my life, I was starting to lose interest in having any real connection with my father. Whenever any of my family members made remarks about him, I would not engage in the conversation.

However, my mother always encouraged me, "Son, I know your father disappoints you by not calling or following through with what he says he'll do. But at the end of the day, he is still your father, whether you like it or not. I know it's a lot to ask, but you could call him every so often."

But whatever respect I had left would very quickly be lost. I remember my father telling my mom and me that he would be coming to see me, but at this point, I was so desensitized to those words that I brushed it off like it was nothing special. But later that day, to my surprise, he showed up. In my head, I was torn between being happy or upset. On one hand, I hadn't seen my father in a while and was glad that he showed up. But on the other hand, I remember the countless times he said he would come to see me and never fulfilled that promise.

One thing I noticed, was that my mother was never really happy to see my father. At the time, I did not understand the exact reason why, but I knew it was something serious. This particular time, however, was different. My mother didn't come to greet him when he walked through the door. Instead, she stayed in her room and told me to let her know when he left.

My father walked in the door, looked around, and asked, "Where is your mom?"

"She's upstairs in her room taking a shower," I replied.

"Go upstairs and tell your mom she could at least come downstairs to speak to me."

"Okay," I sighed.

As I was telling my mother what my father had said, I could hear his footsteps coming up the stairs. *Oh, no*, I thought, *I guess he wants to talk to her himself. I don't know if this will go well.* But everything seemed normal.

They had a quick conversation, but again, I could tell that my mom was annoyed.

So being the curious child I was, I decided to talk to my father myself. I wanted to know why every time he said he was coming to see me, he would all of a sudden either cancel or say he couldn't make it.

"Dad, why do you say you'll come see me when you don't actually come to see me?" I asked. The reaction on his face said it all. I could tell he was scrambling to find an answer.

After a few seconds, he responded, "I've just been busy with work, and other things have come up unexpectedly. That is why I have not been able to see you as much."

I may have been a child, but I was not dumb. I knew this was a lie and not the real reason he was not able to see me.

I was so tired of his excuses, so I decided to tell him what was on my mind. I looked him in his eyes and said, "I do not think that is the real reason you don't make an effort to come see me. I wait hours upon hours for you every time you say you're going to come pick me up. And every time you say that you won't be able to come see me. I am starting to think that I am not a priority for you and that you do not care about me as much as you say you do. I mean every word of this, Dad. This is not something that my mother told me to tell you. This is coming from me, and only me. I don't think it's fair how you have been treating me and my mother as though we are afterthoughts. You've hurt my mom, and you've hurt me. I hope you see now that your actions have affected us more than you've thought."

Both my mother and father were speechless. They did not expect me to say what I did and be so passionate about it, but that is truly how I felt. After that, my mom walked downstairs with my father while I stayed upstairs. Eventually, my father left. That was the first time that I had undoubtedly made my father realize that not being in my life had an effect on how I felt about him.

After this encounter, I could tell my father took what I said seriously as he made countless efforts to call and check up on me. He even came to pick me up to spend the day with me on his days off. This was one of the first times that I actually felt like I had a father figure in my life. I was happy to talk to him and tell him about how school was going and everything that was going on in my day-to-day life. I was glad that we were connecting as father and son.

Unfortunately, all good things must come to an end. Over the years, our relationship started to dwindle like as it had before. There was less and less of an effort to come see me, talk to me, or even contact me, or to see how I was doing. Now granted, I was used to this by now, so it did not impact me like it did before, but I was definitely disappointed that this conflict had made its way back again.

My relationship with my father was at its worst when I made the transition into high school. During that time period, I had only seen my father about three or four times in the last four years. From birthdays to holidays to even big milestones in my life, all of my family was there for me, except for my father. He refused to take responsibility for not being in my life. In fact, sometimes, he pointed the finger at me and said that I was the one who had not made enough of an effort to connect with him. I could never understand why he would even think that way. If I'm not mistaken, I did not ask to be born into this life, although I'm blessed to be here.

Parents have a responsibility to care for and protect their children regardless of the circumstances of the relationship between them and their partner. Now, my family made countless attempts to explain this to my father, but he continued to shut them down and stuck to the way he saw things.

Whenever I spoke to him, he would always turn the situation back on me instead of taking responsibility as a parent.

One day, my dad said, "Look, you're always talking to me about reaching out to you, but you're not putting in any effort to reach out to me either. Why don't you let me know when it is a good time for me to talk to you."

My reaction was the same every time he said this, "Okay, dad, will do." However, I had no intention of doing so because whatever logic he was using was backward. I was not going to try to fix something that was not my fault. And so, as the years went on, I continued to ignore his calls and messages. I had no interest in speaking to my father. This was the start of the fall off.

Throughout my time in high school, I was a very accomplished student. From a high GPA to the president's awards to graduating with honors from a community college while simultaneously earning my high school diploma. There is little that I have not accomplished academically. There were a lot of ups, downs, challenges, and triumphs to get to that point, but one thing remained constant, my father was never there to celebrate my achievements, not once. At this point, he was an afterthought to me. He would say he was proud of me but never really showed me he was true to his word. I've always lived by the quote "actions speak louder than words," and for my father, it was the complete opposite.

Just when I thought it could not get any worse, the unthinkable happened. I needed a new passport because my old one had expired. So, my mother and I were working through the process when we ran into a problem. Since my mother and father were divorced, the court settlement required that both of my parents would have to approve any major decisions that were made for me as long as I was a minor, such as getting a new passport.

So, for the first time in a while, I called my father. When he answered the phone, I explained the situation and told him how important it was. Then, I asked him if he would sign off on a paper stating that he would allow me to get a new passport. Seems simple enough, right?

"No!" he said, "I'm not signing that paper. As a matter of fact, tell your mother not to contact me for anything else, ever again!" Then, abruptly hung up the phone.

Both my mother and I looked at each other, shocked but not surprised. In doing this, my father showed us that he really did not care about me and wanted nothing to do with me. I have felt the exact same way about him for a while, but this was the last straw. From this point on, I decided I would not have any association with him. As far as I was concerned, he was no longer my father.

I have not seen, talked to, or contacted my father in three years. Most people would say that is a long time, but for me, I don't feel any different. I am who I am, and I was dealt the cards I was dealt. Instead of complaining about them and using my misfortune as an excuse, I worked that much harder to ensure that I would not be solely defined as the kid who grew up without a father. I wanted to show that it was possible to only have one parent in your life and still be successful. So, although I may not have had my father in my life, it was his decision not to be in my life. It was not my choice, nor was it my fault. However, it was up to me to do something that my father didn't do—I was determined not to become like him when I entered adulthood. I saw how it affected my whole family, and I knew I had to be the one to break the cycle.

Fast forward to today. I am in college and going to one of the biggest and most prestigious four-year universities in the nation. I am studying finance and have hopes of becoming a chief financial officer of a Big 5 company. I graduated from high school with a diploma and an associate degree in business. I have helped countless businesses with E-Commerce shops, business websites, logos, and much more. Not only that, but I am now an author.

I have accomplished so much already, and my life is just getting started. All of this could not have been done without the help of my family. From my aunts to my cousins to my grandparents, every last one of them has helped me grow into the person I've become today.

However, the most important person in my life is my mother. As a single mom, I could not imagine how hard it was for her to raise a child, practically by herself, especially, after what she had gone through with my father. My mother is the main reason that I keep going. I recognize that her effort to ensure that I have a great life is something she dedicates all of her time and energy towards. The worst thing I could do is take that for granted. So, I make sure with every milestone I reach and accomplishment I receive, I dedicate it to her. She is my everything and my purpose. There is nothing I can do to repay her for all she has done for me, but I will do whatever it takes to make sure she knows how much I love and appreciate her for everything she has given me.

The moral of my story is, "Don't let that one person, moment, place, or mistake hold you down and control your life." I could have let not having a father figure in my life negatively affect my trajectory, but I didn't. Instead, I used it as the motivation to do more and break the stereotype for children living without a father.

Remember that you have people in your life that will always support you no matter what. Whether it is a cousin, uncle, aunt, mother, father, friend, brother, sister, teacher, minister, or other people in your community, there is always someone who will be there for you. I was blessed enough to have a wonderful support system that consisted of friends and family that kept me going despite my situation. Those were the people that I wanted to make proud and impress. Why? Because they were the ones that stuck with me my whole life. Without them, I would not be where I am today.

If you are reading this and you have gone through something similar, regardless of age, sex, or race, I hope that my story has inspired you in one way or another. If you haven't gone through something like this, then I hope my story gave you a different perspective and opened your eyes to something very special. Without a father in your life, you can still survive and accomplish great things!

AFTERWORD

By

Joan T Randall

When I set out on this journey of The Image in The Mirror, I never thought it would have the impact that it has. A quiet prompting from the Holy Spirit led to a three-book series and a documentary film. The Image in The Mirror Trilogy has given birth to 39 different stories, with 37 of these individuals as first-time authors. That is a fantastic accomplishment. What a way to end this series with these Kings.

So often, little boys are taught that they should get back up and never cry if they fall. Or if they are hurting, they should keep it inside and not let anyone see their vulnerability or emotions. But unfortunately, this has given rise to grown men who still carry pain, offense, trauma, hurt, and disappointment in their hearts. And because nurture has shown them to hide their emotions, some men have never dealt with or acknowledged the reality of their feelings.

These seven men disrupted the norm. They share their stories hoping that it will change the narrative of how our society views the way men should react to their emotions. It is not ok to be manly and macho and never acknowledges one's experience or to feel or seek help. Instead, they want boys, young men, and adult men to know it is ok to share what they think or ask for help, and in doing so-the pain can become a lesson in time instead of a ticking time bomb.

So, if you can relate to any of these stories or see yourself in a space where one of these authors was, or if you are in that space as you read this book, do not keep it to yourself. Instead, reach out, phone a friend, talk to someone, and take the necessary actions to see yourself as God sees you.

If you want to write your own story, don't hesitate to contact joan@victoriousyoupress.com.

ABOUT THE AUTHORS

DWON L. FIELDS, Sr.

Dwon L. Fields, Sr. was born in Beaufort, SC on September 14, 1978. Having grown up in Bluffton, he is proud to be called a Lowcountry native. He graduated from Hilton Head High School where he was very active in the Seahawk's athletic department--both on the football field and the baseball field.

Mr. Fields has held a professional position with Beaufort County School District for the past 14 years. For the past 8 years he has been the Behavior Management Specialist for Bluffton Middle School. As the schools BMS, Mr. Fields works with the district staff to help assess and develop a variety of methods to improve student behavior. To further feed his passion for athletics, Mr. Fields is also the Assistant Athletic Director as well as the Head Coach for the middle school Baseball team.

Mr. Fields is a strong community leader. He uses his connections in the community to help whenever and where he sees a need. His biggest motivation is his family. He is a father of one son, Dwon "DJ" Fields, Jr. Despite life's adversities, Mr. Fields still has hope for the youth of the Bluffton community. He strives to be a positive role model. He is the President of his own non-profit--TEAM 55 LIVE LIKE DJ—a foundation dedicated to the memory of his son—in which he desires to use DJ's life story to offer hope and positive direction to young men and women as well as the tools they need to grow into better versions of themselves.

PAUL D. BUSH

Paul Bush was born and raised in Ohio before moving to NC. From a very young age, he had to rely on his own merits, but his relationship with the Lord was the most consistent. After working for the Air Force for several years, he began a career in the financial industry. After a 25-year career in the Financial and Investment industries, he was led to create a financial ministry/literacy company, to reach and teach GOD'S people. Paul's story has always been about the favor of GOD in his life and the miracle of His healing power.

He is a husband, father, and grandfather and currently lives in North Carolina with his wife, Tamra.

JARVIS SWANSON

Jarvis Swanson relocated from Nashville, Tennessee, to Charlotte, NC. He quickly immersed himself into the Charlotte faith-based community to serve and give of his gifts and talents. Jarvis is known for his quiet strength and his professional demeanor. He is the Regional Vice President of Operations at MedData and brings multiple years of experience and longevity to the HealthCare Management arena.

Jarvis is a husband and father and currently resides in North Carolina with his wife, Demetra.

ABRAHAM ANDERSON

Abraham Anderson, number seven of nine siblings, was born and raised in Baltimore, Maryland. He attended Mergenthaler Senior vocational technical High School and majored in Business Administration. He has an Associate Degree in General Studies from Central Texas College, a Bachelor of Science in Psychology and a minor in Management from Columbia College, and a Master of Science in Administration from Central Michigan University.

Abraham served 23 years in the United States Army as a Veterinary Food Inspector, Medical field. His rank of retirement was First Sergeant. After serving in the Military, he became a Junior Reserve Officer Training Corp instructor at Crawford High School - San Diego Unified School District, California, for twelve years. He taught Military Science, Drill and Ceremony, Leadership Development, curriculum requirements, and

Physical Fitness programs as mandated by the San Diego School District and United States Army.

Abraham married his high school sweetheart, Annette Anderson, and together they have three adult children Jamal, Brandon Anderson, and Tiyauna Zambrano. They have been married for forty years and currently reside in Southern California.

JEAN JOHNSON

Jean Johnson's debut as an author is a long time coming. However, the New York native is thoughtful and is always willing to engage in deep conversations when it comes to sharing his concerns on the matters that plague the progress of his people. He has lived in several cities in the South; however, New York City remains the place he calls home.

He attended Julia Richman High School in Manhattan, NY, and Brooklyn College University.

The most important occasions of his life were the birth of his two kids, son Jean (1993) and daughter Jashira (2000).

Jean's prose is thoughtful, emotional, fluid, and transformative. He works in healthcare, and during his free time, you will see him reading, writing poetry, or creating online content.

CHRISTOPHER LEONARD

Christopher Leonard was born on 25 February 1987 in Huntsville, AL, to Scarlet and Wayne Leonard (parents) with older sister Ashley Leonard. He attended Sparkman High School from 2001 to 2004 and graduated from Grissom High School in 2005.

He graduated from Athens State University in December 2014 and completed his education at the Florida Institute of Technology (FIT), graduating in August 2017. He now works in the Defense Industry and has over seven-plus years of experience.

He is a father of 2 young men (Kingston & Alijah Leonard).

JABARRIE MONSANO

Jabarrie Monsano is the Executive Assistant for My Sister Keeper. He is currently enrolled at Louisiana State University on an Academic Scholarship, working towards graduating with a Bachelor's Degree in Finance. In high school, Jabarrie took part in a Dual Enrollment program at Montgomery College in Maryland and, at 17, graduated with a high school diploma and an Associate's Degree in Business.

Jabarrie's life goal has always been to put his best foot forward in anything he does. He strives to help the people that have helped him and always wants to give back to the communities with which he's involved.

THIS BOOK WAS COMPILED BY

JOAN T RANDALL

Joan T. Randall is an independent publisher, international speaker, award-winning best-selling author, and business coach. She is president of Joan T. Randall Enterprise LLC, founder of Victorious You Press, and creator of the Book 2 Business & Beyond® Bootcamp, where she teaches authors to leverage their books to create multiple income streams.

She is a recipient of the Women's Entrepreneurship Certificate from Cornell University. Joan received her certification in Homiletics from Howard University and is an Ordained Elder. In addition, she is a Certified Life Coach, Public Speaker, and Domestic Violence Advocate.

Joan is the Publishing Director for Nehemiah Project International Ministries - a Global biblical entrepreneurship organization that serves five continents and 40 countries worldwide.

Additionally, she is the Co-Executive Director of The Boost Pad, an organization providing underrepresented founders' resources to create solutions, build impactful businesses, and increase economic mobility in Charlotte.

Affectionately known as the author's midwife, Joan Randall helps thought leaders and individuals of faith write and publish their stories, messages, and experiences to monetize their impact and influence, build their businesses, and create legacies.

Her awards and accolades include but are not limited to outstanding community leader, entrepreneur of the year, women's leadership & advocacy, and literary award winner, as seen on ABC, NBC, CBS, and Fox.

Joan was born in Kingston, Jamaica. She is a mother of two and GiGi to four. She currently resides in North Carolina.

www.ingramcontent.com/pod-product-compliance
Lightning Source LLC
Chambersburg PA
CBHW071941210726
48293CB00004BA/1344